MW00778710

WE

REFUSED

TO LEAD A

DYING CHURCH

We Refused TO LEAD A DYING CHURCH!

CHURCHES THAT CAME BACK
AGAINST ALL ODDS

PAUL NIXON

 THE PILGRIM PRESS
CLEVELAND

TO Johnny and Patricia Floyd, who showed up out of nowhere one Sunday morning almost a quarter century ago and helped me to lead Pleasant Grove Church from the brink of death back to vibrant life! It was close, but we made it, by God's grace, and Pleasant Grove is still serving its community many years later. God is good!

SUSTAINABLE FORESTRY INITIATIVE
Label applies to the text stock

Certified Sourcing
www.sfiprogram.org
SFI-00341

The Pilgrim Press, 700 Prospect Avenue, Cleveland, Ohio 44115
thepilgrimpress.com.
© 2012 by Paul Nixon

Scripture quotations, unless otherwise noted, are from the New Revised Standard Version of the Bible, © 1989 by the Division of Christian Education of the National Council of Churches of Christ in the United States of America, and are used by permission. Changes have been made for inclusivity.

Printed in the United States of America on acid-free paper

16   15   14   13   12   5   4   3   2   1

Library of Congress Cataloging-in-Publication Data

Nixon, Paul, 1962–
    We refused to lead a dying church : churches that came back against all odds / Paul Nixon.
        p. cm.
    ISBN 978-0-8298-1895-6 (alk. paper)
    1. Church renewal.   I. Title.
BV600.N49 2012
262.001'7—dc23   2012005048

C O N T E N T S

CONTENTS

INTRODUCTION

It has been five years since The Pilgrim Press invited me to write a book summarizing what I had learned from consulting with more than 250 churches in the mainline American context. That request resulted in a book titled *I Refuse to Lead a Dying Church.* In that book, I unpacked six key choices that leaders of vibrant churches almost always make, in almost all kinds of community settings. The six choices were very obvious to me, and the manuscript just spilled onto the page in a few weeks. I did not expect or predict that the book would become the press's bestselling title the next year. Several times people told me they devoured the thing in one sitting, on one pot of coffee.

So I asked people why the book hooked them. In response I have heard:

- The title grabbed them. It shouted something they feel deeply.

- The book got folks talking in their local church, talking about important things that needed to be talked about!

- The six choices are easy to understand and relatively simple to make—not complicated and not overwhelming.

- The book talks about church health and growth in ways that progressive Christians can easily relate to.

- The book offers hope. It is predicated on the conviction that no church ever has to give up. There is always a way toward life!

I have taught *I Refuse to Lead a Dying Church* from coast to coast, in the North and in the South, with multiple Christian denominations, with clergy, with laity, with city people and rural people. It has really been a lot of fun!

People constantly have asked for real life examples, to know what this choice or that looks like in places similar to the places where they live and worship. This book comes in direct response to these requests. In the following pages, I show you what *choosing life* looks like in some ordinary places where people of faith are experiencing new life together and blessing their communities in significant ways.

In the five years since I wrote *I Refuse to Lead a Dying Church*, I have continually tested what I wrote against new experiences in the following ways.

Each year I engage with a new set of faith communities and leaders, who live out the six choices in brilliant ways! This year alone, my coaching organization, Epicenter Group, will work with the leaders of about eighty congregations or pastoral charges. In each case, we will test ideas and refine ministry practice.

In recent years, my work has taken me from Shanghai to Manila to Toronto, to nearly every corner of the United States. (Christians of the Eastern and Western Hemispheres, and of the right and the left, can learn much from one another.)

A few years back, I packed up and moved to a new part of the United States. I shifted from a regional denominational office in a sleepy Florida beach town to downtown Washington, D.C., to plant a new faith community focused on the needs of urban young adults. It has been a season for learning what it means to do church with people who are two decades younger than I am! (I shared some of this, in reflection on my dizzying first year in D.C., in the 2009 book *Finding Jesus on the Metro*.)

This planting effort ultimately took root in the soil of our community through my partnership with a two-hundred-year-old downtown Washington congregation that shared a similar vision. In 2010 we launched "Sunday Night @ Foundry" (SNF). It is a worship community designed for some of our neighbors who were rarely—if ever—going to show up at any church on Sunday mornings. SNF is a new community, nested within a very old one, the Foundry United Methodist Church. It is steadily growing, with a multiethnic mix and a median age in the low thirties: a virtual mirror of our neighborhood. It has been one of the richest ministry laboratories one could ever hope for!

After all that I have seen and questioned and tasted in these years, the six key choices still feel sound and in sync with my experience of diverse healthy congregations. I stand by them:

1. Choosing life over death

2. Choosing community over isolation

3. Choosing fun over drudgery

4. Choosing bold over mild

5. Choosing frontier over fortress

6. Choosing now rather than later

But exploring actual stories takes us from two dimensions to 3-D IMAX. The fifteen stories in this book move beyond the tidiness of tightly crafted ideas that may feel so comfortable in a world of change. They also move closer to reality. These fifteen real stories are windows to complex, living communities, each with much more to teach us than we can summarize in this limited space. You will recognize each of the six choices in the pages ahead. But you may also discern other patterns and, in certain respects, the lack of pattern. I will draw conclusions here and there, but many more can be drawn. I invite you to draw them.

Let the stories speak for themselves. Let the Spirit speak between the lines. Chase it wherever it goes!

As I began the research for this book, I approached it almost like a contest to find the most amazing stories of the "fifteen best church transformation tales in America." I announced my search for great stories and invited nominations from judicatory and denominational leaders across the United Methodist Church, the

United Church of Christ, and the Presbyterian Church USA. Many of the churches in this book came to my attention via judicatory and denominational leaders. A couple came to my attention because they are in my neighborhood.

But the more I looked, the more I was confronted with amazing stories—in all directions—in all traditions. They are each beautiful in so many different ways. How exactly could any human being—or even a blue ribbon committee, with limited information and finite wisdom—judge winners? They are all winners—and so many more besides them! These are churches, after all, not contestants. They are communities of people, beloved by God, who exist to worship God and to serve their neighbors.

So I reframed my task—and began to focus on the ordinariness of the churches and their leaders.

These are stories of ordinary people whose churches were in trouble, where something changed, and then almost everything changed! Some of the churches were near death. Others were just stuck in old patterns, so that few could imagine a different reality.

In each case, they chose life, and lived into a miracle. They each chose to take community seriously. The leaders of each stepped up to the growth required in them to lead effectively. Each church partnered laity and clergy constructively and creatively. They each experienced the mystery of Spirit movement. They each came to moments when they refused to look backward any longer, but chose to face forward, to keep moving, and to trust God. Eventually they all had fun, though often not at first! Some of the folks who went through the transformation at their church offer brief encouraging remarks or directives for others attempting to turn things around in their own churches; these are included as "postcards" at the close of most of the chapters.

In no case did any of these places become a megachurch. Megachurches can write their own books. I was looking for stories you might otherwise never hear, and stories that may be closer to your reality. I would hope that one or two of these stories might jump off the page for you and ignite your imagination. I would expect that there is something here for almost every church. But I would also expect that certain stories might not relate so well to you. You may be surprised as to the ones that capture your interest. So please do not discount a story based on denomination, region of the country, or other factors. Give each a chance. Read prayerfully and be surprised!

You will notice that these faith communities do not live out of a single playbook. There are multiple pathways to renewed congregational life.

- These churches understand the Bible differently.

- Their pastors lead differently. One of the places is not clergy-led at all.

- In at least three cases, laity became the major drivers for change and innovation.

- In one case, the breakthrough came in a pastor's second decade of tenure in the congregation. That's unusual, but obviously not impossible.

- These churches thrive in different parts of the United States, in big cities and smaller communities.

- They reflect the varieties of church size dynamics in terms of how decisions are made and how change takes place. Six of these faith communities still gather less than a hundred people for worship each week.

- Several of them experienced painful congregational conflict on the road to new life. Other churches embraced their journey to life more easily.

- Some of the pastors really suffered, in order to lead faithfully, almost like mothers in labor. Two pastors had their lives threatened as a result of their leadership and/or their congregation's ministry. One battled a life-threatening illness in the midst of her work. One went through a divorce. I would expect half of them went to therapy.

- Quite a few family members of the pastors carry scars from these church transformation experiences. Some of them left organized religion. In other cases, the whole family's faith grew stronger.

- Old, historic (and often dysfunctional) buildings hinder some of these faith communities and help others. The fastest growing of the fifteen has no building at all.

- Some of these churches witnessed dramatic transformational moments, like a Texas "blue norther" in autumn that knocks the temperature down forty degrees in an hour. Others experienced new life like a gentle fall breeze in Virginia, creeping in steadily and without much fanfare.

- In a few cases, the denomination offered real help along the transformation journey. More often than not, the denomination neither helped nor hindered the church's decision to live.

- About half the churches have adopted official statements of welcome to gay and lesbian persons. In others, such hospitality is lived without making a big deal of it. And in still other places, the leaders harbor serious concerns about homosexuality.

Despite this diversity, I do not present these to you as a snapshot of diversity in American religion. All but one congregation is associated with historic Protestant traditions with European roots. There is one story of a Jewish synagogue that has as much to teach Christians as any other story in the book.

This book is designed for study with clergy groups, local church groups, denominational groups, seminary classes, and others. If a group of laity from a single church desires to study this book together, please invite your pastor into your study group. Little progress ever comes of this kind of conversation when the pastor is out of the loop.

As with my other books, there is a free group study guide available at www.epicentergroup.org and also at www.thepilgrimpress.com. I encourage you to download it and to reproduce it freely. It will help you use this book for reflection in a study group or retreat setting. You can follow it closely or just borrow a few ideas. In any case, it should prove helpful to you in seeking to craft a constructive conversation with fellow church leaders.

The first such conversation is shared briefly in the last pages of the book, where four Christian leaders chat with me. These persons have each devoted many years to helping congregations choose life. They reflect with one another on what big ideas or themes struck them in the stories.

- CHARLENE KAMMERER retired in 2012 after sixteen years as an active United Methodist bishop with her most recent area of service, the three-hundred-thousand-member Virginia Conference of the UMC. She is also my bishop!

- CHRISTIE LATONA consults with churches and denominational teams around ways to choose life and grow ministry. Christie and I work together as co-leaders of the Readiness 360 movement (www.readiness360.org).

- MARTIN LEE is director of Congregational Development for the Northern Illinois Conference of The United Methodist Church, which includes the Chicago region.

- RITA ROOT is interim Conference Minister for the New York Conference of the United Church of Christ, which includes the entire state of New York.

ㅎ

1

THE RENEWED TALL STEEPLE CHURCH

Calvary Baptist, Washington, D.C.

Cultivating a brilliant future in the shadow of a magnificent yesterday is a rather common theme in twenty-first-century congregational development. We begin with such a story, based about four blocks from my home in downtown Washington, D.C.

During the early 1860s, with the first Republican elected president and no nonpartisan civil service yet in place, there was a significant turnover in Washington's population as the Lincoln administration set up its operation. Washington was flooded with more antislavery folks than it had ever seen before. The war began. The city of Washington sat in a precarious, almost indefensible location, surrounded by states where slavery was legal. Many people lived with the constant worry that they would have to flee the city on short notice before Confederate troops burned the place to the ground.

If managing the long-running tension between abolitionist and proslavery sentiment had not been enough challenge for the E Street Baptist Church in D.C., just add the war, the new wave of Yankees, and the fear that everyone would soon lose everything! So several of the most ardent pro-Union folks left the church in 1862 to form a new congregation, Calvary Baptist. If the city fell, some felt the new church might not last a year.

After the Union victory at Gettysburg, to get on with life, people in D.C. settled down and began to trade real estate again. In 1863, members of the young Calvary Baptist Church bought a small plot of land on the corner of H and Eighth Streets NW, in what was projected to be the hottest area of development after the war. Today it is known as Penn Quarter. The neighborhood lay between the White House and the Capitol. One block south of Calvary's land, the new Pensions Building (now the Smithsonian American Art Museum and Portrait Gallery) was arguably the most opulent building in the city, anchoring a new wave of upscale development. Two blocks west was Mary Surratt's boarding house, where John Wilkes Booth and the conspirators hung out (now a sushi bar). Penn Quarter would become the heart of downtown Washington in the late 1800s, with major commercial corridors in several directions weaving all around the church.

After the war, Calvary grew quickly, due in part to a few wealthy individuals who gave generously to erect an amazing building. Within their first decade they had twice constructed a grand Gothic building (the first one burned soon after completion). This is the same building where Calvary worships today, a large red brick sanctuary with a magnificent pipe organ and an ornate wrought-iron steeple that towers above the surrounding buildings. In the 1890s a horseshoe balcony was added, increasing the seating capacity to twelve hundred (based, of course, upon somewhat skinnier people in that era). Calvary continued to expand its facilities into the 1960s, until the complex stretched from H Street almost to the Portrait Gallery.

At the turn of the twentieth century, Calvary recorded more than sixteen hundred members and an average Sunday school attendance of nearly one thousand. In the early 1920s, a young woman named Jessie Burrall (in a day when women could not be pastors) gathered upwards of a thousand persons a week in her Bible class at Calvary. The President of the United States worshiped regularly at Calvary. The church (or several of its members), almost literally, ruled the world.

In 1907, the Northern Baptist Convention, which later became the American Baptist Churches in the USA, was organized at Calvary.

By World War II, the ushers were packing twelve persons into pews built for ten, with many others gathered in overflow rooms, listening to the service over the PA system. Mass choirs overflowed. More than two thousand attended Sunday school. In the late 1940s, membership peaked at thirty-six hundred and the church held two morning services to accommodate attendance. Scores of folks experienced a call to pastoral ministry here across the years. The church ordained its first female member as a minister in those years. Calvary was well known for its pastor's intentional mentoring of young seminary graduates.

I belabor all of this to say that Calvary Baptist was not an ordinary place. It was a legendary place—was one of the most dynamic Protestant congregations on the planet up until about the middle of the last century. For several decades, it was in a league with the Riverside Church in New York City

But communities change. And congregations are rooted in community. The Calvary neighborhood, known by several names across the years, has changed significantly about every forty years. For decades a strong German community lived alongside folks of British and Irish ancestry. Then with the post–Civil War renaissance, a strong Jewish community came—many of the leading merchants of old Washington. They came, and then they went (as we will see in another story in this book). In the 1930s the D.C. Chinatown was forcibly relocated from Pennsylvania Avenue several blocks north to H Street, bringing in Asian residents. After World War II, when the suburban building boom began in Maryland and Virginia, many of Calvary's members moved to more modern homes on larger lots. Membership began to slip, and then to plummet. For the next half a century, Penn Quarter was an African American majority neighborhood. By the 1980s, as their members also moved to safer neighborhoods with more modern homes, some of the stronger middle-class black congregations in the neighborhood relocated to the suburbs. The community grew poorer. The regal row houses along Massachusetts Avenue were abandoned, torn down, and turned into parking lots. Through all of this change, Calvary stuck it out.

Clarence Cranford, the legendary preacher who packed the house twice each Sunday in the mid forties, watched the crowds thin substantially in the 1950s, and even more through the 1960s. When he supported adding the church's first black member, Florence Davis, to the church membership in 1955, there was much grumbling. By a slim margin, the church accepted her. Dr. Cranford's resignation letter was ready in case they did not. By the early sixties, Dr. Cranford was discouraged, and he accepted a call to a church in Maine, near the Cranfords' summer home. After the move, however, Mrs. Cranford suddenly died. Dr. Cranford missed Washington. So Calvary called him back at the end of the same year. He stayed through a tumultuous decade. (Even into the twenty-first century, elderly members would often invoke Dr. Cranford's name as they made various points about the good old days, or the way that things should be done.)

The 1968 riots finally did to downtown Washington what folks had worried the Confederates would do a century earlier! Many of the downtown congregations came near to collapse in the 1970s and 1980s as legions of long-time residents left for the suburbs.

Grumbling is common in declining churches. Rifts and dissensions became more frequent at Calvary. The gigantic buildings began to fray and sag. When the Gallery Place metro (subway) station opened in the mid-1970s, one block from Calvary, government offices to the south used to provide security escort for workers to and from the trains. The neighborhood was by then a mix of boarded-up buildings, second-rate Chinese restaurants, dying churches, a few liquor stores, and an occasional porn theater. It was a depressing atmosphere.

This was the nation's capital city, however, and a few visionary Washingtonians saw what others could not—that this was still the heart of Washington, D.C.! They believed that Penn Quarter could rise from the ashes to become the economic and entertainment heart of the region again. Quietly these visionaries began to buy real estate. In the early nineties, a basketball/hockey arena, now known as the Verizon Center, opened near Calvary. This building did to the neighborhood what the Pensions Building had done 130 years before: it anchored a new wave of development, and with the development came a new influx of people. On the heels of the new arena, a new D.C. convention center opened two blocks north of Calvary. Then came the condos and luxury apartments for government workers. After forty years, with a daily influx of people, came the retail outlets, plus chic restaurants and nightclubs. By the 2010 census, Penn Quarter had the fastest population growth rate in the city, with soaring numbers of white-collar residents. Crime was dropping steadily. Seedy businesses were almost extinct. And each year, the gentrification wave continues to move about a block or two further to the north and east, far beyond Calvary, now enveloping Logan Circle, Shaw, Bloomingdale, and Eckington neighborhoods—all places where Calvary people used to live.

To understand the renaissance of Calvary or of other nearby congregations, it is important first to note that a new city was built here in the last twenty years, on the foundations (and ruins) of earlier communities that thrived on these same streets.

By the late nineties, the neighborhood momentum had turned, but most of Calvary's members still would not live to see the new city that was about to emerge. Quite a few wondered if the church itself would live to see this. Members from that time described this to me as "a time of great uncertainty." Much congregational energy was consumed with the maintenance of the buildings. The church was land rich and cash poor. One of the last major funding campaigns of that era led to a total renovation of the pipe organ, making it again one of the finest organs on the East Coast. So they had a world-class organ and almost no people.

The church was *steeped* in heritage—*haunted* might not be too strong a word! They clung to the ways they had customarily done things, organized for a world long passed away. They were largely clueless about the future. According to Pastor Amy Butler, "The faithful people who sat in the pews on the corner of H and Eighth Streets, NW, were determined—if it was the last thing they did— to concentrate on the task of getting things back to the way they used to be when everything was going so well at Calvary."

The church did remain relatively community-oriented even during their leanest years. Several significant social ministries were started in the seventies and eighties, especially with the children in nearby neighborhoods. Calvary's commitment to such ministries helped to attract members who cared about urban issues and people. But the overall numbers of participants in the core ministries of the church continued to diminish. Only a handful of members now lived within a mile of the church, compared to a couple thousand members within walking distance a half century earlier!

At the turn of the twenty-first century, soaring property values opened an opportunity for Calvary. Between its southernmost building and the Portrait Gallery, the church owned a dingy sixteen-car parking lot. They struck a deal with a developer, selling him the parking lot in exchange for the following:

- A parking garage would go in where the sixteen cars had parked, four levels underground, providing four times as much parking space, with greater security, protected from weather, and with a direct elevator entrance into the Calvary facility.

- An office building would go up above the parking garage extending over and above two of the existing Calvary buildings.

- Proceeds from the sale would finance a total renovation of Calvary's facilities, with $3 million left in a fund to help support operational expenses for years to come.

In 2003, as this construction commenced, the church called Amy Butler from the Saint Charles Avenue Baptist Church in New Orleans to be their tenth senior pastor. Neither she nor they had any idea what they were getting into. Despite the massive building renovation underway, the church was only two funerals away from losing about half its operating income, and just a few more years from losing the vast majority of those who remained active. Something had to change, or Calvary Baptist Church was going to die, fabulous pipe organ and state-of-the-art Gothic building notwithstanding.

The next few years were tumultuous. Some in the congregation were uncomfortable with a female pastor. Amy Butler was the antithesis of the legendary and oratorical pulpiteers who had welcomed some of these folks into membership decades earlier, backed by a hundred faces in the choir. Amy's gender, her generation, her personal style, her theological center were just different, even disorienting!

Some people in the congregation were, mystically, *still at church with Dr. Cranford*, in what was now an imaginary world.

Imagine, if you can, the neighborhood around megachurch Willow Creek Community Church (outside Chicago), changing in its mix of people, and the church going down, down, down to almost nothing over the next fifty years. And then imagine a young bright pastor in the year 2062 coming to lead them, a young woman who does not look like, talk like, think like, or act anything like Bill Hybels, Willow's pastor. You get the idea.

One of the gifts to Amy, as she started to lead Calvary, was that the building plans were already in place and underway. This kept her from having to spend several months mired in the nitty-gritty of meetings with committees and architects, designing a building and a business plan.

She started with sixty folks in worship, most of whom would be gone by her fifth year. So in terms of building the congregation that would exist in 2008, she really started with about two-dozen in 2003. The Sunday crowd was eclectic and disconnected. When they moved back into the renovated space, they sat themselves down all over the cavernous sanctuary, *everywhere but the middle of the room*, some in little tribal clusters and others in isolation. The Burmese folks over here . . . the Latinos over there (bussed in on two church vans) . . . the white octogenarians here and there . . . and a handful of new folks scattered about them.

The seating patterns mirrored a deeper sense of disconnection of the worshipers with one another, with their pastor, and with their ministry territory. The emptiness in the middle of the room powerfully symbolized the lack of a coherent middle, a common ground. That coherent center had to be built, painfully at times, across several years. In some respects, Amy Butler planted a new church on the corner of Eighth and H, in the middle of an ancient and magnificent space, alongside grumbling, disconnected refugees from an earlier time and place. The glorious Calvary Baptist Church that I have taken some pains to describe was gone. It had died before Amy ever got to town.

What remained were, in Amy's words, "files and files stacked in the archive room on the third floor." In some respects it was the remnant of a church, and in other respects, the ruins. And even when the remaining few mobilized to deliver food to those who were grieving, just the logistics of getting casseroles shipped from loving sisters across a city of five million people was a nightmare.

The building, though fresh and largely reengineered, was still gigantic, and expensive to maintain. Amy says, "It was nice that someone in the church in 1920 thought it good to build a full-sized stage, outfitted with a red velvet curtain and a full spotlight system, in yet another large hall in the church building." But what do you do with it seventy-five years later? Then someone heard on NPR one day about a local nonprofit that helps kids to sing and perform, which had found itself homeless due to cuts in the public school budget. Fresh thinking led to a partnership with children's theater and, in time, with a myriad of other nonprofits, serving hundreds of Washingtonians. And these people began to traffic in and out of Calvary's building.

With regard to nonprofit partners in the building, the church chose them carefully. There were, and are, three rules: (1) Is their mission compatible with our mission, so that in working together both of our efforts are strengthened? (2) Are they financially stable and well managed? (3) Are the people in charge people whom we would want to call colleagues? (In other words, do we like them?) With this sort of thinking, Calvary moved far beyond simply renting space to other organizations as many churches do—but they really became collaborators with powerful organizations that made Washington a richer place.

In addition to these collaborative relationships, Calvary rented some of their space to another church on Sunday evening and to the nearby Sixth and I Street Synagogue, whose services were overflowing its facility capacity on Fridays and Saturdays.

With the energy of a new young pastor who took great care about her preaching, attendance at the Calvary Sunday morning service bounced back up over one hundred pretty quickly. But the new young apartment and condo dwellers in the area are relatively transient. So with older members passing away, it took a steady influx of new folks simply to replace those who left.

Add to this the grieving on the part of some older members over what in fact was the death of the Calvary they had known. Their grieving attached itself, in unhealthy ways, to various issues, including these:

- Introducing Spanish into the main Sunday worship service for prayers and liturgy caused anxiety.

- Spending into the endowment more aggressively than was originally planned so that the church's rebirth would not be undercapitalized caused further controversy and ongoing fixation on finances.

- An attempt to restructure the church's governance met with shrill resistance from a group of old-timers who felt that the church's soul was at stake in the form of its decision-making processes. A few actually carried copies of the church constitution and bylaws on their person, in little bags, for months, during the controversy over proposals for a simplified governance structure. (The progressive folks wisely chose to back off this particular fight and to live more gradually into a simpler way of being church.)

- A church staff member was theologically opposed to a female pastor. His parents were also influential members of the church.

In early 2006, during year three in Amy's tenure, the unhappy staff person began to stage a coup, culminating in his messy resignation and his parents leading a crusade to fire Amy. Hateful and hurtful things were said. Twenty-six theses or accusations against the pastor were presented to the church council. Behind closed doors in the winter of 2007, the council formally considered all twenty-six accusations. (These items ranged from questioning the pastor's faith to the accusation that she was a workaholic and neglected her children, to the accusation that she did not work hard enough.) The council chose to consider each individual accusation rather than ignore them. This was not an endorsement of their plausibility. When the council rejected all twenty-six, they were able to send a stronger statement of support for their pastor than they otherwise could have accomplished. Calvary was ready to move on. The whole season of mutiny took about eighteen months and was exhausting for all involved. By the end of this ordeal, Amy was exhausted and her family stressed, and she was not sure that she even believed in God—since her belief in God had always been mediated by an experience of the resurrected Christ in community.

Yet it was the defining year of Calvary's resurrection.

After 2008, the church began to move forward more easily, less obsessed with and hindered by the weight of all I have just described. That was the year that the middle of the sanctuary began to fill in. Young professionals continued to come in, even during the worst year of conflict. As was the case in a couple other stories in this book, the negative voices were not well connected to new people in the church. So the constant rehearsing of all that was wrong with the church and its pastor was somewhat quarantined to a dwindling circle of people. That same year, after intentional study, the church approved a statement of inclusion for lesbian, gay, bisexual, and transgender (LGBT) people. It was followed quickly by an inclusive marriage policy—preceding (by two years) the vote by the D.C. city council to legalize gay marriage.

As Amy recovered from it all, she leaned on her associate pastor Leah Grundset. Leah was able to keep leading as Amy processed the pain of it all. The end result was that Calvary did not lose a beat. They rallied around Amy, and they continued to diversify and steadily to grow.

Under Leah's leadership, the church began to develop small groups for study and relationship building across the metro area. They got to seven groups, and then took a sabbatical, backing up to two groups, freeing up energy and space for different forms of study and fellowship. Leah shared that "your small group friends are the people who will meet you in the middle of the night at the ER." Downtown D.C. is made up of people who have located here from all over the world—many are lonely and missing the communities that nurtured them in other places. Washington, D.C., is a political town, with lots of cocktail parties and networking get-togethers, where folks have mastered the art of frivolous chitchat. But, Leah shares, "in a city of facades and anonymity, to be truly known is a powerful thing. So Calvary is specializing in offering possibilities for authentic community for folks."

Leah observes, "Once people are in a deeper community, the real person emerges. The real person, not some party persona, but the real deal! When people really love you, you dare to come out of your shell and give the world the real you."

From 2008 to 2010, Amy would ask, in all sorts of gatherings, "Who here is in a small group?" Finally, in a church meeting, an older woman raised her hand. Her husband said to her, "You aren't in a small group." "Yes I am. I am in the Women's Missionary Society." The WMS was around long before Calvary's small groups, but this woman had recast an old association in terms of a new day in her church, and reframed her missionary society as a part of Calvary's future rather than simply as a great part of its past.

Calvary's community now surpasses two hundred worshipers on most Sundays. Almost all the faces are new within the past five years. For a while the church had been a mix of very old people and very young people, but now the middle—in terms of age—is also filling in. The negativity is now marginalized, almost extinct. Amy's preaching and pastoral energy is rising steadily. I have watched her for four years, and the thing I notice lately is that she sparkles. She has worked to take care of herself and her family through the traumas of the past decade. She seems the stronger for it, and better at what she does.

Calvary made it past the deaths of the two big donors, all the while diversifying and growing their donor base. A large chunk of their operating budget still is supported by accumulated funds and the interest generated. Calvary will probably have to double again in size in order to be able to sustain their ministry financially for the long-term. But good momentum is present, and the chance of continued growth is very strong.

Penn Quarter is extremely diverse in terms of race, social backgrounds, and faith traditions, with a very high percentage of residents being nonreligious as a conscious lifestyle choice. This is, after all, downtown Washington: full of the brainiest of the brainy, and young adults from a generation that is highly suspicious of or oblivious to organized religion. Within the shrinking base of persons who will consider going to church, a large majority tends toward evangelical theology and emphases. Several of D.C.'s strongest churches are full of young evangelicals, including a conservative Presbyterian congregation that meets in Calvary's building on Sunday evenings. But Calvary is clearly poised to relate to the other 85 percent of the population. Many of the latter have been turned off by more conservative religion or by the political initiatives associated with conservative religion. The people who continue to come into the life of Calvary share that they are looking for community, for spirituality, for a church that is aligned with justice.

The term Baptist continues to present challenges to a local population that has been trained by the media to associate this term with narrow fundamentalism. So they use a tagline under the church name: "A different kind of Baptist."

Last Easter, Amy recounts how the baptismal pool almost did not fill due to old pipes, how one of the mentally ill members cussed out the associate pastor at the top of his lungs during the "passing of the peace," and how the fire alarm went off just as folks sat down in the fellowship hall for Easter dinner. (The fire alarm regularly malfunctions.) She was not happy. It was not the Easter she had imagined and planned. But after they got two hundred people outside safely onto the front sidewalk, she looked around.

"There they were, the whole Calvary family, enjoying the sunshine together, passing babies around, posing for pictures in Easter finery. I heard folks chatting with passers-by on our busy city street, inviting the firefighters to join us for worship some Sunday, and laughing together as those who had been around longer told newer members about that time when Pastor Amy was preaching and the fire alarm went off right at the end of her sermon . . ." She adds, "Everybody is still talking about the Easter Sunday fire alarm, but I see the smiles and I can hear the pride in their voices . . . . We know who we are now, and we embrace it."

POSTCARDS FROM CALVARY

- Find what you really value and go with it!
- No one size fits all—know who you are and what your mission is!
- If something doesn't work, don't panic. Just try something else!

- Don't be afraid to shake things up!
- There is no one right answer to any challenge or situation.
- Work hard at being community, at talking to one another.
- In moments of conflict, talk face-to-face as soon as possible. Love each other. Get through it.
- Somewhere in the mix, you need a visionary, who helps to generate new thinking, who sees outside of the box.
- When someone comes up with something crazy, say YES!
- Before you get frustrated, try the craziest thing you can think of and see what happens!

2

THE GOOD NEWS CHURCH

Evangel United Methodist, Holton, Kansas

Holton, Kansas, is the antithesis of Washington, D.C. It is a Mid-western county seat in northeast Kansas, surrounded literally by cornfields. The population has been, give or take, thirty-four hundred people for about as long as anyone can remember. You grow up in Holton and you know everybody in town.

Holton is rural, but it's only a half hour's commute from Topeka and an hour from the northwest suburbs of Kansas City. So the people who grew up here are within reach of good jobs in the event that they want to spend their lives here and raise their kids here. If it were much further to the west, the town would likely dry up. But Holton is hanging in there. During the recent economic downturn, the unemployment rate in Holton ran about half the national average.

Holton has ten churches. (There were eleven churches until recently when the Presbyterian Church USA congregation closed.) Historically, the Evangelical Church in Holton was always one of the strongest in town. It is older than the town. The Evangelical Association was a small denomination of German pietists, especially strong across the American midwest. Through a series of denominational mergers, the church became part of the Evangelical

United Brethren (EUB). Fifty years ago, Holton Evangelical United Brethren Church was *the* flagship church for its judicatory region. Pastors stayed for long tenures. The church was considered the pinnacle of a talented pastor's career. Regional conferences were often held at the church.

And then, in 1968, the Methodist Church and EUB denominations merged. Overnight, the church (changing its name to Evangel United Methodist) was one of two United Methodist congregations in a town of thirty-four hundred, and not even one of the largest twenty churches in the new Kansas East Conference of the UMC. Thus began an identity crisis that would last for several decades.

As with Calvary in D.C., Evangel was haunted by bloated and sentimental memories of a long-lost pastor. In this case, it was Reverend Bill Tudor, who pastored seventeen years until his retirement in 1982. As Rev. Tudor left, he told the congregation that, in the new reality, they were just another church among hundreds, and they no longer could command the highest quality pastoral leaders. He was trying to be helpful, but this statement resulted in a conclusion on the part of many that the glory days had ended with the departure of Rev. Tudor.

Between 1982 and 2007, weekly attendance declined from 325 to 186. Money got tight. Morale deteriorated. Negativity began to flavor church meetings and conversations. Younger faces became scarce on Sundays.

In 1991, the church completed the last building of its campus, its Family Life Center (recreational multipurpose building). They did not yet understand the power of such a facility as a driver for community ministry. It stayed locked up much of the time, reserved for church groups and members.

In 2001, there was a slight up-tick in attendance when the church launched a second worship service with a more "contemporary" format in the Family Life Center. This service, called Life Journey, started after a year's worth of conversation, planning, and anxiety. People were afraid that having a second Sunday morning

worship service would divide the church family. Many were concerned that the music was outside the traditions of Evangel. The
pastor pushed it on through, and then dealt with considerable
drama in the aftermath of this decision. Some were upset that the
service was created too quickly—as if a year is too fast—and without considering the feelings of older members. The bishop's response to this commotion was to move the pastor quite suddenly
to another parish.

Even with the instigator of the new service seemingly abducted
from the church, the new service survived. Life Journey continues
to this day (and currently is thriving). Evangel's next pastor was a
very conciliatory, nurturing man. He worked hard to help people
process their feelings and anger—and to create an environment
whereby the new service could be retained. He was able to gently
and calmly make the case that if they closed the new service, it
would only serve to deeply offend even more of their core folks and
intensify the church's slow decline. So they papered over the conflict and the two worship communities began to live in begrudging
coexistence. Gossip and negativity were constant.

When Kent Rogers came as pastor in 2007, he found a church
lacking a clear sense of self-identity, purpose, or vision. They were
just going through tired motions, without a clear sense of what difference any of it was supposed to make in their lives or in the community around them. Without a clear purpose (beyond making
themselves happy), it became difficult to make decisions except on
the basis of "this is how we've always done it" or "this is what suits
our tastes." When churches make decisions in such an environment, my taste will eventually offend yours, and conflict will arise.

People outside the church could see this more clearly than
those on the inside. Evangel folks took their church bickering to
the grocery store, to the civic club, to the bleachers at the ball field.
This was a small town and everybody got the point, that Evangel
(which means "good news") was bad news. So almost no one new
ever visited the church. When Kent Rogers arrived, he had already
heard the church's reputation far beyond Holton as a church that

fought their pastors. At that time, lay leaders in the church felt the denomination did not take them seriously nor listen to them. The more negative the place got, the more that both the town and the denomination just blew them off.

Upon his arrival, Kent made a gutsy call that would either become the basis of a church transformation or the reason for a one-year tenure. For the first six months of his pastorate, Kent decided that he would, essentially, shine a mirror at the church and show them what they looked like. In this reflective stance, he then asked the congregation what they wanted to become. In his first sermon he asked, "Do you want to be a great church? Because I am not going to accept anything less!"

Within a few months of Kent's arrival, the church began hosting a series of home meetings. Members were invited to visit with one another and their new pastor. More than two hundred folks attended these gatherings—a number that exceeded the church's normal worship attendance. In these conversations, Kent asked the following questions:

- Can you tell me briefly (in one minute) who you are?
- What does this church do well?
- What is the biggest challenge or opportunity that this church faces?
- If you could make one change to this church, what would it be?
- What is on our doorstep that we have not yet seen? (This question was to take the focus of the conversation toward the wider community.)

Kent said that the conversations confirmed that the church had no vision and no clear sense of purpose. The church was busier than ever, but the activities had become unhinged from the true reasons that many of them were started, back when. In thinking about how best to make this case to the church, Kent briefly floated the idea of bringing the old man, Rev. Tudor, back to preach one Sunday. Since many folks saw near-divine attributes in their former pastor, Kent figured that Rev. Tudor would have credibility to corroborate the current discoveries and help to point them forward. Several of the church's leaders, however, disagreed. They felt this would only serve to take the church back in time rather than challenge them to look forward. (This was a critical juncture, where the competent counsel of lay leadership who knew the territory and the history helped Kent lead.)

So Kent gathered all the notes shared at the home meetings and sifted through them with a few leaders. In the late fall, he approached the church administrative board with a proposed vision statement in the form of a short mantra: *To change lives and our community—one person at a time.* They also changed the church name—not in an official action, but in everyday usage—from Evangel United Methodist (usually referred to as EUM) to simply Evangel, putting the clear focus on the point that this was to be a place of good news. And they reorganized. Radically.

The reorganization was quick. It was not drawn out through a lengthy study process. Basically, the church's key functions were boiled down to six teams that flowed from the church's mission statement (which they call a challenge statement). The Evangel challenge is: *To invite our un-churched friends, relatives, associates, and neighbors to experience Jesus and fun and fellowship in the Evangel community of faith, nurture them to Christian maturity, and equip them to serve in the church and community in order to celebrate and proclaim God's name.*

From this, the teams are (1) Inviting, (2) Fun and Fellowship, (3) Nurture, (4) Serve, and (5 and 6) two Celebrate teams, each leading one worship service.

Kent selected two co-leaders for each team, and in turn the co-leaders drafted ten people per team to make up the core of their team. Each group of twelve was commissioned *to have fun together,* to build their team's vision, and to process biblical teachings and foundations related to their team. Six teams of twelve meant that seventy-two people were invited into leadership. But the focus of these teams was *doing ministry* rather than endless deliberation, ar-

THE GOOD NEWS CHURCH

gument, and decision-making. Then the remainder of the church membership was divided up into six groups of forty, each assigned to a particular team. These persons were to be considered "resource people," a first line of potential workers and helpers for tasks and initiatives that the team would sponsor. The teams were challenged to offer at least one opportunity for each of the forty, so that everyone would be invited to come on board during the course of the year. Leaders encouraged each team to think creatively about how to do this.

The administrative board became a church council—a smaller, more centralized decision-making group that kept a big picture perspective—and made as few decisions as necessary. Meetings shifted to a simple format where the six teams reported what they were doing. It all happened with lightning speed. Some folks were unhappy with this new meeting format, and a few left active positions of leadership.

But Kent proposed more than simply changing the leader culture at Evangel. He proposed a shift in the church's culture of members and visitors. Like most churches, Evangel had become a place where members enjoyed privileges that outsiders were not allowed to enjoy—until they too joined. Privileges ranged from high pastoral care expectations for member families to reduced fees for renting church facilities for family functions. It was a bit like a religious country club. So they decided to flip this to a culture where guests could receive any service that the church offered either for free or for the same cost that would be extended to a church member. Guests would get privileges. And members would get a more serious set of expectations. Focus would be on the service and sacrifice that membership entailed. This commitment was developed into a six-point covenant of member behavior that ranged from intentionality in their personal faith journey to the practice of financial giving based on a percentage of their income (growing toward a tithe of ten percent of their income if they were not already there). Additionally, the teams developed specific commitments and values appropriate to their responsibilities.

All of this was very ambitious for the first six months of a pastoral tenure. But attendance and morale began to rise in the latter half of 2007. Kent's honeymoon status as a new pastor enabled him to pull off much of this change.

But there was not one new member in the first six months that Kent Rogers was pastor. Not one. Even in a small town, this is odd for a church Evangel's size. There were very few visitors. The church had isolated itself over many years of inward focus and fussing. Yet Kent did something that I have never heard any pastor do in her or his first sixth months in a place: Kent told the church, "Don't invite anybody yet. We aren't ready yet." He named the fact that they were not ready, and that they needed to get ready for guests, for company. It wasn't as if members were inviting neighbors anyway at this point. The new teams, the community focus, and the inviting would commence in 2008.

And then something happened that no one could have scripted, but God.

In December 2007, an ice storm hit northeastern Kansas. About an inch and a half of freezing rain settled onto houses, roads, power lines, and trees. More than a million homes in the region lost power, including everybody in Holton. For some residents, two weeks and several more inches of snow would come and go before power would be restored to their homes.

Without calling any meetings or taking any votes, Evangel went into action. They checked on neighbors and they power-sawed tree branches to open up roads. Most of the town would be without power for a week. But, because the church was on the main line, its power came back on the next day. While the rest of Holton was still shivering in the dark, Evangel's church building was now warm, with light glowing through the windows—so they spontaneously flung open the doors and welcomed in the town.

First, they offered their building to the Red Cross. and it became the official Red Cross center for the week. The denominational insurance would not cover them to house people unless they were a Red Cross center. Kent said, "Make it happen." This was one of the first instances where the church recognized a situation where ministry was within the boundaries and mandates of what they existed to do. So they just did it. No permission was necessary—people were clear that they had been empowered to "do whatever it takes."

Meanwhile, officials from the city and schools were waiting on permission to work with the Red Cross. While they waited for approval and decisions, Evangel just jumped in ahead of them and did it. Evangel took the community lead. People from both worship services came together working side by side for the next week, bringing all the work of the first five months into real time ministry. They served hundreds of meals that week to their neighbors and made scores of new friends—deep, meaningful encounters, hours of coffee conversation and laughter. Fifty area residents slept in the church's classrooms. Kent nicknamed the place the Evangel Hilton.

After the storm, everything was different.

Attendance on Sundays began to exceed three hundred again in 2008. It has steadily grown every year since. Looking at the story from a distance, it was almost as if Kent Rogers had come in with a defibrillator and, within six months, administered electroshock. The result was a church resurrected and looking healthier than it had looked in years. Two critical things happened—first, with the no-nonsense focus on mission and excellence, the church managed to reclaim a high percentage of its inactive folks. Second, the ice storm probably accomplished in one week what could have taken years—it convinced Holton, Kansas, people that Evangel was a good news place.

In some respects, it is easier to keep track of inactive members in a small community than in a metropolis. But small town dynamics had also worked against them, establishing a poisonous reputation on the community grapevine. Evangel had a bad brand in Holton. And branding perceptions in small towns are hard to shake in a day.

So let us all thank God for the special opportunities that come with really bad weather!

The next three years brought several new families into the church along with the families of folks who had grown up in the church. And these younger adults, in keeping with the spirit of their generation, are passionate about making a difference in their community. Their generational instincts played right into the transformation already underway. Because the church had continued the controversial Life Journey service, they were ready to quickly integrate these new families into church life. The service grew in number and in the quality of music and visuals. In addition, the Family Life Center became Holton's busiest community center.

The church resurrected a children's choir (a choir that had existed in the Rev. Tudor era) called Today's Tomorrows. The choir started in the fall of 2008 with the hope of attracting a dozen kids, and by 2011 the enrollment was approaching a hundred children from all over the county. There are now two children's choirs: kindergarten through second grade, and third to fifth grade. Both groups meet on Wednesday night for food, fellowship, and singing and to become deeply committed Christian disciples.

In 2009, the church raised $100,000 for major cosmetic work on its buildings, built between the 1920s and the 1980s. The main entryway into the building was redecorated and renamed the Link. Adjacent to the Link is a new coffee shop called Sacred Grounds, complete with a flat screen TV and gourmet drinks. (Remember, Holton is a small town that has not yet seen its first Starbucks—so the coffee shop brings value here in a way that may not be true for every place.)

The people of Evangel understand that this church is not theirs, but that it belongs to God and exists as a resource to the community. The members are simply stewards of the resource.

Meanwhile, Kent Rogers has looked for ways to be a pastor to all of Holton, and not just to Evangel. On Friday nights in the fall and many nights in winter, Kent is the "Voice of the Holton Wildcats." In a town this size, such an opportunity to announce high school football and basketball games is pure gold for a pastor and worth all the time it takes.

Perhaps the most salient demonstration of the Evangel's commitment to the wider community is the church's growing engagement with Hispanics in their county. Hispanic workers are especially attracted to jobs in a local meat packing plant. In a part of the United States where many folks see Hispanics as intruders, Evangel is trying to love their neighbors and to welcome them. The fact that many of Evangel's forebears were once German-speakers in an English-speaking land may make this easier. "Do for them what was done for us." This new ministry focus first bubbled up in the home meetings. It is rooted in the church members' family history, in their passions and awareness. This makes it all the more powerful.

The bishop will likely soon appoint a bilingual associate pastor to Evangel, so that they will be able to more fully include all of their neighbors. The preliminary thinking is that this new pastor will be able to devote about three-fourths of his or her time to reaching and serving this new population, and the other one-fourth of the time tending to existing systems and services. The new faith community is called Nueva Vida (meaning New Life).

Evangel's engagement with the Hispanic population goes far beyond recruiting them for church services. Recently a young man moved to Holton from Los Angeles. Local law enforcement officers kept stopping the young man and asking for identification. Recognizing that many of their neighbors are undocumented and essentially voiceless in public life, the people of Evangel have determined to be their voice. So now church members are standing up as advocates for the civil rights of their Hispanic neighbors.

This is very good news. It's Evangel.

POSTCARDS FROM EVANGEL

- Look to Jesus' ministry. It was controversial. It rocked some people's world. Why should we have it any easier?
- God is still at work. And God usually gets God's way!
- If it can happen in a stagnant change-resistant place like Holton, it can happen anywhere!

- You can be where we are today or be where the Presbyterians are. (The PCUSA church in Holton has closed.)

- Come talk to us! We'd love to show you what we're doing! (Twelve churches have visited us in recent months to learn.)

- Do nothing ordinary.

- Make a choice—will you be a "whatever" church or a "whatever it takes" kind of church? Evangel's leaders have chosen to do whatever it takes.

- You better get busy living! Otherwise you are just waiting to die!

3

THE REBORN CHURCH

Hope.Gate.Way, Portland, Maine

Chestnut Street Church was dying. Everyone knew it. The season of denial was long past. There was so little traffic in and out of their building that many in the community assumed they were already gone.

Located in downtown Portland, for decades Chestnut Street was the flagship church of the Maine Conference of the Methodist Church. The church began in 1795, as Methodism exploded through the state of Maine. Built in 1857, its sanctuary is still standing and in good condition. It was the site of innumerable Methodist conferences and home to the first church organ in American Methodism. Chestnut Street was the home congregation of the legendary Deering family, who moved west in the 1870s to help build Chicago. Across the years, this was an amazing and influential place.

And yet, most good things come to an end. By 2000, the church was winding down fast. Like Calvary and Evangel, Chestnut Street lived in the shadow of a magnificent history, which made their current reality all the more discouraging.

The Chestnut congregation entered its third century debating whether or not to sell the building and move to a new location. The argument went on for years, unresolved. The old facility was located on a low-traffic downtown street. It had neighboring buildings on both sides, causing it to have poor street visibility, except when you were right in front of it and looking for it. Additionally, the building maintenance costs had become untenable.

By 2005, worship attendance had fallen to the thirties, in a room that could easily hold 700. The congregation wasn't getting any younger or any larger. It made sense to sell the large building and move into a smaller, more manageable, more flexible facility.

But the sanctuary was extraordinary, both architecturally and historically. So letting go was not going to be easy. Some, of course, believed that letting go of the building meant the end of the church—a familiar issue. The church and the building were so intertwined in their minds that it was difficult to imagine a Chestnut Street beyond their historic Chestnut Street building. And so the decision kept getting postponed, and church membership kept diminishing. During this era, pastors came and went quickly., Most just maintained things and held services for the few who showed up.

Finally, by the time church leaders seriously examined likely sale proceeds and the cost of land and construction, they discovered that they had probably waited too long. Further complicating the idea of selling and moving, the bishop announced that he wanted to keep a church downtown.

In 2006, congregants of Chestnut Street took the leap and sold their historic property to a developer. With the loss of the building, they also lost about half their remaining people. They moved worship services to the nearby Etz Chaim Synagogue. In 2007, their average worship attendance slipped to thirteen. People recall Sundays when it dropped as low as six, not even a *minyan* in Judaism (the minimum number to function as a synagogue is ten).

Just after they vacated their historic home, another dying church, Westbrook, explored merger with Chestnut. The merger did not work out but the conversation was apparently helpful for the Chestnut folks. Westbrook had just gone through a discernment conversation related to their future. They brought a sense of reality and purpose to the conversation with Chestnut at a time when reality was overwhelming and purpose still a bit fuzzy. Westbrook folks modeled hopefulness, spiritual adventure, and follow-through. A few Westbrook folks stayed, while most others moved on to other churches. The larger witness of the Westbrook contingency, however, may have become a key element in helping Chestnut accept reality and step with God into its new future.

Most of the remaining members were retired social service professionals, whose careers had ranged from social work to nursing to teaching to ordained ministry. Although they were small in number, this remnant was a feisty and forward thinking group. They could so easily have just thrown in the towel. But that was never an option. Nor were they content to just hold on until the last funeral. These folks cultivated a genuine vision and desire for their church to serve downtown Portland.

In 2007, Bishop Peter Weaver visited them at the synagogue to learn more about their thoughts on the situation and to make a proposal. Memories of the meeting are a bit fuzzy, and versions vary. Bishop Weaver was a bit vague, but he gave them some hope. People mostly heard what they wanted to hear. Everyone heard him say that if they were serious about pursuing a bold future, he would appoint someone with the gifts to lead into that future. Some people heard him propose a new church plant alongside the existing church. Others heard that the new pastor's mission would be to revitalize Chestnut and they would become the new church.

Oddly enough, regardless of how they heard it, all of the aforementioned possibilities eventually came true.

Later that year, the bishop sent a young clergy couple, Allen and Sara Ewing-Merrill, to Chestnut. Allen and Sara had only been out of seminary a few years, but they were already counted among the most promising young clergy in the region. This was to be a challenge, however, far surpassing anything Allen or Sara had experienced before.

The major reason that Chestnut Street and many other churches had fallen was that Portland had simply changed—and not as much demographically as culturally. There was never a dramatic demographic shift, such as occurred in Boston or Philadelphia. The interior neighborhoods of the city were, of course, older and housed more low-income families, even some immigrants. But the historic and picturesque nature of the city invited constant reinvestment, renovations, and gentrification. Today downtown Portland is charming—the Arts District, the waterfront, the lovely old homes—on the surface this would seem like a community where church development would be easy.

The developer who bought Chestnut's building sold it to a restaurant group, which renovated it into a two-story, high-end eatery, complete with gourmet food presentations, stained glass windows, and a bar in the middle of what had been the nave. The church parking lot became the site of a new loft condo development. Obviously, the economy was pretty good on Chestnut Street.

Downtown Portland never deteriorated economically like many American cities in the mid-twentieth century. Nonetheless, Portland experienced an epic shift—from being a highly churched city to one of the most unaffiliated communities in the United States. The shift paralleled what happened in Canada and in Scandinavia during the latter half of the twentieth century: the Christian culture simply collapsed. Volumes have been written analyzing how this occurred. For our purposes, I will simply note that no other story in this book has been written in a territory more ideologically hostile to organized religion. I have compared the difficulty of Allen and Sara's work to that of church planters in Stockholm and Copenhagen.

Actually, Allen and Sara were sent to Portland with a mandate to plant a new faith community alongside the Chestnut Street congregation and to nurture both as sibling congregations. The new church community was named New Light. The funding for this endeavor was made possible by a portion of the proceeds from the Chestnut Street property sale. Additional proceeds from the sale helped the two faith communities secure a small facility and establish operating cash for several years as they built a large donor base to support the ministries.

In the early days, Chestnut people expressed mixed feelings about New Light. One member shared, "It was like a new baby brought home by the parents to an older sibling. We were jealous, anxious, and afraid that our needs would not get met." Some Chestnut people hoped that all the New Light people would start coming to Chestnut. Others feared that New Light would get all the new members. A few people clung to the misperception that Allen and Sara were sent to close them down—this was never the case, but once the idea lodged in certain minds, it was always a part of the terrain. "They were New Light, and by deduction, that made us Old Light."

In late 2007, Chestnut was still worshiping at the synagogue, with about eighteen to twenty people. New Light was taking off slowly, as a sort of house-church with a handful of folks. The big challenge on everyone's mind at that point was to find a permanent place to call home, which both churches could use as a base for their ministries.

At the same time, the three years spent in the synagogue offered a rich "wilderness time," which gave the church time to grieve, to discern, to let go, to imagine, and to begin to re-form. If they had moved directly from the Chestnut Street building into a new building, it could too easily have become a Chestnut Street Memorial and Museum rather than a ministry center designed for a new community. After this wilderness time, Chestnut Street people were no longer a culture of memory with a fortress mentality, but a culture of the present, looking for new opportunities to serve and adaptive to change.

They put a big map of Portland on the table and evaluated various parts of the city. The Parkside neighborhood, adjacent to the Arts District, stuck in their minds and hearts. It was the densest square mile of population north of Boston, and there was no United Methodist ministry presence there. Parkside tended to be a hard-living area, and with the social services mentality of the Chestnut remnant, this made sense as a place where there would always be great opportunities to serve others and to make a difference.

In March 2008, four persons (two pastors and two laity) traveled from Portland, Maine, to Sheffield, UK, on a learning mission with a group called the Urban Theology Unit. Over the course of a week, they went on multiple field trips to ministry centers and churches that had done unique things with their buildings. They saw a wide range of social ministries. They were especially impressed with the Desmond Tutu House in Bradford, England, led by a young Anglican priest, oft arrested for protesting this or that. In the process all of this ministry exploration, they engaged in deep conversation about a different vision of church—as a center of community life, invested in transforming both community and individuals on both the inside and the outside.

Upon returning to Portland, they found a thirty-five-hundred-square foot office suite situated on the street frontage of a relatively new parking garage. It was a good location, on the border between the downtown Arts District and the Parkside neighborhood. They bought and renovated the place, and creating a very modern and airy space with large meeting rooms, a gathering area, gift shop, small office and kitchen, and a children's area. The walls are covered in local artist's work, all for sale. On first Friday nights, when the downtown sponsors its monthly Arts Walk and all the galleries are open, this facility is on the map and open as well.

Since two different churches would use the space, the leaders decided on a neutral and "unchurchy" name. The one selected was Hope.Gate.Way.

In 2009 and 2010, New Light continued to develop very slowly, mostly around a strategy of home fellowships. They developed three such groups. They tried a monthly Sunday evening worship service for a while, but it never caught fire. Meanwhile, on Sunday morning, a few New Light folks started showing up for worship at Chestnut. Attendance began to creep up into the thirties, then into the forties. Additionally, the Chestnut folks began showing up at New Light events. Community outreach projects became joint efforts. In July 2009, the churches voted to become a Reconciling Ministry, explicitly offering a welcome to LGBT folks.

In the fall of 2010, the idea arose to just rename the whole system of ministries Hope.Gate.Way. Increasingly, this was the term that people used to refer to their church—since it was the physical place where they would often gather. They phased out the terms Chestnut (which pointed people to a street where they no longer gathered) and New Light (which was also confusing to community people, who knew their facility by another name).

The New Light faith community had not yet chartered as a new congregation separate from Chestnut. So the renaming in effect served as the merger of the two communities.

They soon began a second Sunday morning worship service. The meeting space began to feel full with fifty attendees. With two services, they could keep growing. In the spring of 2011, Hope.Gate.Way began to surpass seventy in attendance many Sundays. A definite sense of momentum and success began to shape their community life. Because the space is intimate, and community relationships are valued, they describe the "Passing of the Peace" as a full-contact sport in which everyone is greeted by at least two dozen people. Worship gatherings are lively, joyful, and interactive. In addition to Sunday worship, four weekly home groups (called Life Groups) meet in various neighborhoods. A growing cadre of small children is prompting serious energy and focus on creating a new initiative in children's ministry, appropriate to Portland and within the culture of Hope.Gate.Way.

Allen is convinced that the Chestnut Church could never have made the necessary choices and created the space to attract the dozens of young adults who have come in without starting the revitalization as a separate stream of community life cordoned off from the more institutional culture of the older church. Almost everyone is convinced that none of the church growth would have happened if they had not created and cultivated Hope.Gate.Way as a center for community life in the neighborhood.

The relatively small facility limits the kinds of activities and services that can be offered. However, all the space is multipurpose and it has daily people traffic. It is clear that most of the new ministries and activities will be based outside the church facility. Nevertheless, having an attractive small building as home base continues to offer stability, identity, and efficiency for the church's community life.

The community meals program—not a lone endeavor but a partnership with Wayside Food Kitchen—was the first major community initiative offered at Hope.Gate.Way. Eight thousand meals were served the first year. This program offers an opportunity for church members to volunteer, but it is not entirely dependent on them. Thus, it is not a trap for volunteer burnout in this still relatively small congregation.

The cooperative meals program helped to raise public awareness of Hope.Gate.Way as a servant organization. It also helped Hope.Gate.Way folks to get to know a good number of community people living on the economic margins. They began to see anew how so many of the challenges in people's lives were rooted in drugs, alcohol, and mental illness. As of this writing, they are exploring how to partner with programs and ministries related to substance-abuse recovery. Possibilities include art, meditation, and support groups.

It is highly likely that five years from now, this ministry will have expanded far beyond what can be told so far. But the farther into the future that they develop, the more difficult it will be for certain other endangered New England churches to see that this model offers creative ideas and options for their future.

Money remains challenging. The financial resources of new members are limited. The pastors estimate that if everyone gave 20 percent of his or her income, the church still could not pay for the ministry from weekly collections. So they are still living partially off proceeds from the Chestnut Street sale. Without those funds, none of their successes could have happened. The church has a few more years to grow, to develop new sources of revenue, and to share costs before they will operate in the black.

This church may yet grow to be a sizable and formidable force in southern Maine or it may remain a relatively small congregation with a vibrant worship life and dynamic connections to transformational ministries throughout the community. In either case, it should be noted that this has not been an easy project—not a story of "Build it and they will come." But the people of Hope.Gate.Way, both the Ewing-Merrills and the key leaders of this church have toughed it out. They are now seeing the first fruit of that investment.

And, in case you missed it, Chestnut Street Church isn't dying anymore.

POSTCARDS FROM HOPE.GATE.WAY

- Do not try to be something other than what you are. Be authentic!
- What we are together is better than what we are separately.
- We had to confront our fears and grieve our past before we could embrace our opportunities!
- Having a great time! Wish you were here!
- Church should be fun!
- Don't be afraid of the people outside your doors! Let them in!

Allen, who offered the last "postcard" in the list, expanded on his message to tell the story of a homeless man, often intoxicated, who would urinate in front of the new building. When Allen saw him the other day, he thought, "The man just needs to pee. That is not a crime." So he let him in for a few minutes to use the restroom. Allen summarized the experience in three words: "We let people in."

4

THE VITAL MERGER CHURCH
United Christian, Austin, Texas

There is no city in America with more interesting demographics than Austin, Texas. I was born here fifty years ago, and despite my love-hate relationship with my birth state, I can't help but love Austin. Back in the early sixties, Austin was about a fourth of its current size and Lyndon Baines Johnson's family still owned the only major TV station, the mighty Channel 7. In those days, the community revolved around two major industries: state government and the University of Texas (UT). Both of these entities attracted highly educated staff. And this clustering of so many highly educated folks in a midsized city began to shape the personality of Austin in distinctive ways.

In the mid-twentieth century Austin had a tradition of strong liberal and moderate Protestant churches, with a high value for the ecumenical movement. These churches existed on an ideological island in an otherwise largely conservative-fundamentalist region of the country. The legendary Carlyle Marney preached at First Baptist downtown in the 1950s. By the early 1960s, philosopher Charles Hartshorne at UT was in his prime, developing a view of reality that would prove foundational for the development of Christian process theology. Nearby, at the Episcopal Seminary of the Southwest, Paul Van Buren was in his heyday, applying linguistic analysis to Christian faith statements, producing what the media dubbed "the death of God."

This was all before the Austin music scene came of age. Austin's formidable technology corridor hardly existed. The world had yet to discover the many colorful and vibrant bars on Sixth Street. Austin was just beginning to collect its first hippies. The bumper sticker "Keep Austin Weird" was still a few decades out into the future. But Austin was a bit weird, at least for central Texas even fifty years ago.

Perhaps the most normal thing going on, in a Texas sort of way, was the continued behavioral patterns and social structures of racial segregation. These habits and behaviors worked together to cluster the majority of African American and Hispanic residents into a couple of ghettos in the east central part of town. In the late 1800s, Austin's racial diversity was spread somewhat evenly across town. By 1950, however, most folks who were not white were corralled into a single quadrant of the city. As the population of this quadrant grew, the people from those neighborhoods would soon overflow into adjacent neighborhoods.

All of these dynamics play into the story of United Christian Church.

Two new congregations were planted in the new middle-class residential section that grew up in northeast Austin after World War II. This new, mostly white community was to the north of Austin's historic black and Hispanic neighborhoods. On the western end of this area, just east of Interstate 35, lies the Windsor Park neighborhood, where Trinity United Church of Christ was located. On the eastern end is the Pecan Springs area, where Pecan Springs Christian Church (Disciples of Christ) was located. Historically Pecan Springs was the larger of the two churches. In the 1970s, African American folks began to settle in Pecan Springs, and Hispanic folks in both neighborhoods. The Trinity and Pecan Springs churches grew older and smaller as kids graduated and moved away. A few of the old-timers recall going door to door in northeast Austin in the early 1980s and not finding one person interested in their church.

Today, in the area around Pecan Springs Church's original location, about one in ten persons is non-Hispanic white; in Windsor Park, about two in ten. Given the cultural realities of Austin, both of these congregations would now be long extinct had the following events not occurred.

During the 1980s, their two denominations, the United Church of Christ and the Disciples of Christ, engaged in national discussions about possibilities for shared ministry. The leaders of Pecan Springs and Trinity began talking and a plan emerged. The two churches agreed to merge, come up with a new name, sell both properties, and find land somewhere on the north side of the city to rebuild and start over again. The talks progressed fast—maybe too fast—and before they knew it, United Christian Church was born in 1991. The church aligned itself officially with both the UCC and the Disciples.

Theologically and socially the two predecessor churches were fairly similar. Members were mostly white, middle-class folks, with grown children, slightly leftward in their views on things, and comfortable in a small-church culture where the role of laity was valued highly. The biggest difference between the groups was their practices of sacraments. Pecan Springs immersed people and shared communion every Sunday. Trinity dribbled out water in sprinkles when they baptized, and they observed communion once a month.

As they sought to craft a unified congregational life and culture, compromise was the main operative principle. They kept both of their pastors for a year. Then both had to leave, in keeping with their "prenuptial" agreement. The church chose the smaller building of the two, in the more visible location. They sold the larger property to a growing black church. Pastor Tim Tutt, who did not come along for ten years, explains that the early years were a time when they developed "two ways of doing everything from baptism to blowing their noses."

The Trinity people were older than those attending Pecan Springs, and they sometimes felt as if Pecan Springs' members pushed them around and manipulated church matters to always get their way. During the interim period before the church called its first pastor, the question of how to handle communion almost unhinged the merger. They decided to take a church vote on how to celebrate communion. Sensing that the conversation was not moving in a constructive direction, the interim pastor stood and said, "Look, I really don't think Holy Communion is something we should vote on. Let's just do it every week." The congregation was so shocked that they agreed. For the next few years, through a five-year pastoral tenure and beyond, it was table tennis—the last pastor was this, the next one will be that. Last year we did this; next year we'll do that . . . and so forth. An older pastor was later called who helped to hold things together for about five years—during the years of dreaming "What next?" and "Where next?"

In 1997, about the time that the church sold the Windsor Park property (to yet another thriving black Baptist church), the pastor of five years retired. He did not have the energy for the rigorous journey of moving the church to another part of the city. When, yet again, the church went into pastor-search mode, it was time for a Disciples of Christ pastor. But no clergyperson could be found who either fit the church or was interested in taking on a small congregation that met at 8:30 AM on Sundays in a borrowed Lutheran church building. So for three years, United Christian worked with an interim pastor. It was a time of serious consideration of their mission, which they boiled down to "Loving God and neighbor."

They chose the high tech area of North Austin for their new location, on a major cross street, about half a mile from the MoPac expressway (named for the Missouri Pacific rail line it parallels) that cuts quickly north-south through the city. They were able to pay cash for the land, using proceeds from sale of previous facilities. They had cash to pay for part of construction, but not all. They would need to take out a loan for a good portion of their first building. Had they tried to do this in the banking environment of a decade later, they might never have pulled off this move.

Thankfully, a denominational agency was willing to loan $800,000 to a scrappy congregation of thirty-five worshipers. Denominational affiliation can be helpful at times. It plays a significant role in about half the stories in this book. United Christian did not receive a grant in this case, just a loan. But had there been no loan, I would probably not be telling you this story.

In 2001, just a few months before construction was complete in North Austin, United Christian Church ran across Tim Tutt. Tim was neither UCC nor Disciple. He was a young progressive Baptist serving a small congregation in Washington, D.C., as associate pastor. His Baptist congregation was in the process of merger with a neighboring United Church of Christ congregation. Tim was a graduate of Baylor, a hundred miles north of Austin. After college he had worked on Capitol Hill as a congressional staffer. He felt a call to pastoral ministry and went to seminary part-time, while continuing to work part-time in Congress. As a person from a third denominational tradition, Tim was able to help United Christian Church become something more than an alliance of two historic traditions (or factions)—to really become a new church.

Dirk Elliott, a United Methodist church developer in the upper Midwest, defines a process called Vital Merger, in which two or more churches

- merge as one
- choose a new name
- organize on the basis of mission rather than survival
- sell all of the former facilities
- secure a pastor who is suited and equipped to lead them into a new future as a new congregation
- create a new life in a new place

This process has a much higher rate of success than normal mergers when the vitality and positive momentum of the merged congregations is measured five years into their new life. Rather than the merged church shrinking in the first five years to the size of the larger predecessor congregation, vital mergers usually show net gains.

The story of United Christian is a Vital Merger in slow motion. Perhaps due to their congregational polity and the lack of significant outside push, their process of merger, visioning, real estate deals, and leadership selection took them a full decade. The leadership selection adventure involved five pastoral good-bye parties (requiring use of church punch bowls) followed by four pastoral welcome parties in only ten years! Many very fine churches in such a situation would never have survived to see their tenth birthday, let alone move into a beautiful new facility on a major road on the growing side of the city.

There may have been only thirty-five regulars left meeting at the Lutheran Church by the year 2000, but they were an exceptional thirty-five. These were the ones with staying power—willing to stick it out, see it through. They were spiritually alive and ready. There was no playing church for ten years. Neither was there wistful longing for the 1950s to make a surprise return. This little church was wrestling with the gospel both personally and in their life together.

They had all the reason in the world to be discouraged. Few pastoral candidates saw them as a worthwhile investment. The same could be said of the lenders, when they looked at the project. But these folks had the kind of faith that could survive the Dustbowl. One member, Chris, who was on the journey all those years, says, "We never panicked, but it was a scary time! We barely had adequate resources day-to day." Another member, Elizabeth, reflects, "We had discussions about whether or not the church would really make it."

The actual time where they nested with the Lutherans lasted nine months, basically the time of construction. Mention of this fact surprised some of the veterans of that era (which was only a decade ago). It seemed to them like it must have been two or three years!

Pastor Tim arrived in June 2001. Seventy people showed up for worship that day, the most in several years! Three months later they moved into the new building with ninety in attendance. And it just grew from there. Launching worship with ninety people in a suburban location in Austin, Texas, still represents a very low number. It is below what we would usually consider "critical mass" for a suburban church plant. But it was so far above what they previously had and their spiritual energy was so strong that nothing could hold United Christian back after September 2001—except perhaps to have chosen the wrong pastor. (Every church in this book lives by grace, but none more than United Christian!)

They chose the right pastor. Bulls-eye. They nailed it. They found what they needed. They specifically chose to move beyond the normal denominational channels when no adequate pastoral candidates surfaced in those places. Rather than put up with the best they could find, they changed the rules in order to find the best they could have! (If you are from a church system with congregational polity, please reread the previous sentence several times, and pray.) They did not lower their standards in any respect, not educationally, not theologically, but they widened their search. At one point, the search committee was worn out from taking multiple long trips to see people preach—and with no breakthrough. So they passed the baton to another fresh committee, saying, essentially, "You all see what you can do." A dynamic layperson in the church became the chair of the new committee, the one that found Tim. Ironically, after the committee found Tim, this man and his family moved to Washington, D.C., at the same time the Tutts moved to Texas. Their cars passed somewhere in Tennessee.

As Tim arrived in Austin, he received all-too-common advice from one of the denominational senior statespersons: "Do nothing the first year." (I cannot believe people are still handing out this advice. This is not even helpful advice for a rural church in Pennsylvania.) Tim reflects, "Holy Smoke! That would have been a disaster." He hit the ground running. I asked some United members for one-word descriptors of Tim. "Manic." "Wired." "High energy." "Dedicated." "Lovable." "Giving." "A leader."

The enthusiasm that Tim engendered from this patient group of saints who had been huddled in the Lutheran wilderness, coupled with the opening of the new facility and the flood of new faces week by week starting in the fall of 2001—it all made for an amazing beginning for Tim's pastoral journey with the people of United Christian Church.

As they consider the last ten years and the amazing growth of their congregation, now approaching three hundred folks on campus many Sundays, they recall the following milestones:

- Just after Tim came, they hired a new music director, Lauren Zachry-Reynolds. Lauren is classically trained, as is her pianist husband. Both work for the University of Texas Music School by day, and they are often found in smoky jazz venues by night. With their help, the church started a fifth Sunday jazz service in 2001. With a grant from the Center for Transforming Worship, they expanded this to a once-a-month jazz service a few years later. It is very Austin, very cool. (They see jazz as a metaphor of what church is supposed to be: improvisational, redeeming the mistakes, organic, and coming home to the melody.) Anybody who wants to sing can find a place to do so—there are groups and ensembles. The sound ranges from classical to world music to gospel. Every Sunday is a surprise.

- One day, a lesbian couple came by the church wanting to join and to have their baby baptized. The older women of the church were very excited to be able to throw their first baby shower in years and to use the punchbowl for something besides a welcome/good-bye party for the minister!

- Pastoral interns came alongside Tim to give the church more leadership capacity, one of whom was "out and lesbian." She invited plenty of her friends.

- In 2006, the church voted to become officially Open and Affirming. This fit well with the church's progressive social views and ease in welcoming gay and lesbian members.

- The church added classrooms and remodeled the sanctuary for greater human accessibility and openness.

- The children's ministry has grown to about seventy-five kids on most Sundays, with more than a hundred on the roll. There were sixty-eight children in Vacation Bible School last year, with another forty leaders. Additionally, a youth fellowship has now developed with middle school and high school age students. Seventeen youth went on a summer mission trip last year.

- On Sunday mornings, Pastor Tim invented one of the most creative children's sermon spiels I have ever seen. He cooked up this mythical character called Malachi Mouse, who purportedly lives in the church building and talks to Pastor Tim early on Sunday mornings. Tim will say each week, with the children gathered, "I was walking through the church this morning, and I heard a little voice say . . . " And the children and congregation respond in unison: "Tim Tutt!" To which he says, "And I said . . . " Then in unison again, "Malachi Mouse!" And then Tim moves into a tightly formed five-minute teaching time with the children, where he tells about some conversation with the mouse, in which, for example, the mouse asks, "Why are the paraments purple today?" Tim goes to great lengths to learn the name of each child and to call them by name. Malachi Mouse time is often the favorite part of the service for both children and adults.

- The church added another associate pastor, giving the church three pastoral leaders at any given time.

Most of the people who come to United Christian come from what Tim calls the "church alumni association." They dropped out over the years because church was boring, dull, or exclusionary. When many of these folks have children, they begin looking again for a church, wandering in with the question "Is this place safe enough to bring my family?" These are people absolutely disgusted by TV religion and by most megachurches, especially with the political associations of such ministries these days. United's people come from various denominational origins, most from families with some Christian history. The openness to LGBT people seems to be as important to the straight folks as the gay ones—for many this has become a signal issue as to a church's openness and commitment to justice. United's people also come looking for a relatively traditional worship experience, an experience with historic hymns and some liturgy. "Traditional but not stuffy" is how Tim would put it.

They are smart—eight librarians, thirty-plus public school educators, several UT professors and grad students, six seminarians, and plenty of young families with small children, all looking for a progressive Christian alternative.

United has been rich in terms of lay leadership from the beginning. Today, fourteen (lay) elders are available to lead the communion prayer (each Sunday) and to lead shepherding groups. Elders check in with folks, pray with them, and keep up with pastoral needs. There is a permission-giving environment, encouraging innovation by anyone who sees a need or wishes to form a new group. If you have an idea here, just sell it to a couple of others and go for it! The church has social justice groups, environmental stewardship (green) groups, service groups (such as Stephen Ministers), fellowship groups, education groups, and discussion groups.

United reaches a segment of people that most of Austin's churches are not prepared to serve. And it is all because a few folks hung tough for a few years in the wilderness, with a dream of what could be, by the power of God.

Meanwhile, the Nineteenth Street Baptist Church and the Mt. Sinai Baptist Church are both thriving in the former locations, doing far better ministry than the people of United Christian could have done in either spot. Mt. Sinai has grown so that they are now in process of moving to their own new plot of land further north, where they will have thirty acres to spread out. It is sometimes easy to criticize churches that move due to changes in neighborhood ethnicity, especially given the history of racism in places like Austin. But in this instance, it looks to me like Austin is better off because the people of United Christian Church passed their previous locations on to people who were better equipped to serve those neighborhoods. They found a new place where they could make their best spiritual contribution to Austin—and they are making it!

POSTCARDS FROM UNITED CHRISTIAN

- Take some risks—don't wait until you have it all figured out!
- Be of good courage and do it.
- Dynamic leadership. Right location. Involved congregation.
- Determine your strengths and build on them to get unstuck.
- Don't be afraid of a little debt. (If we had been afraid of debt, we'd still be paying for the lot!)
- You have to extend your friendships to everybody!

5

THE TURNAROUND CHURCH

Wollaston United Church of Christ, Quincy, Massachusetts

This is a story that some readers may already know in part. The rebirth of Wollaston UCC formed the basis of the book *The Turnaround Church: Inspiration and Tools for Life-Sustaining Change*
(Mary Lou Gifford, Alban, 2009). Their story stands out in particular because of how they attracted grants from a range of organizations as strategic leverage for their rebirth.

Wollaston Hill is a historic neighborhood of Quincy, Massachusetts, an inner-ring suburb, about seven miles south of downtown Boston. The community is nearly four hundred years old,
dating back to some of the earliest European settlers in New England. This is the place where, in 1636, Anne Hutchinson settled, and
where she became one of the first female preachers in America. In
the 1700s this was the place where John and Abigail Adams lived.
In the late 1800s, the community was subdivided into lots for fine
residential homes, becoming one of the earliest commuter suburbs.
From Wollaston Hill, workers could ride the Old Colony Railroad
straight into the city of Boston.

During this redevelopment in what was, already, a 250-year-
old community, a group of residents organized the Wollaston

Congregational Church in 1876. Between 1915 and 1925, they erected a stately Gothic Revival building. It looks like an old village church from England. The octagonal stone tower and high slate roof are as impressive to passers-by today as when the building was built. The same could be said of the stained glass for those who worship inside. Yet, as is often the case with historical properties, the maintenance issues on the building are enormous, with a half-million-dollar laundry list of somewhat urgent structural fix-its accumulated at almost any given time.

The church surpassed nine hundred members briefly in the 1950s, quite large for a neighborhood church. The pastor in that era was one of the movers and shakers in the creation of the United Church of Christ.

Over the next fifty years, as the community population turned over, the church became increasingly disconnected from the heart-beat of community life, to the point where they had only about two dozen active members left and enough money to last another two or three years before they would close. They went from a full-time pastor to a part-time. According to one neighbor, "We thought they were already closed." There was virtually no midweek activity and just a handful of older folks in and out for an hour or so on Sundays.

The neighborhood retains a charm and a sparkle, even as the families who ruled this hill for generations have mostly moved away. Many of the grand old homes are now divided into apartments or condos. The population around the church today is ethnically about one-fourth Chinese, with the remainder mostly white and American-born. The white people who attend old-line Protestant churches in the community is at an all-time low. People tend to be unaffiliated, Catholic, nominally Catholic, or non-denominational Protestant, in that order. A new church plant related to the Vineyard movement meets in a nearby school with as many congregants as several of the historic churches combined. Meanwhile the Chinese American population more than doubled in the last decade and will increasingly help to define the flavor and culture of the northern neighborhoods in Quincy. The Boston Chinatown Neighborhood Center is now developing a satellite location in Quincy.

Mary Louise Gifford came to this little church as pastor in 2003. At the age of fifty-three, she was fresh out of divinity school, a rookie in search of her first pastoral call. In her career prior to this point Mary Lou had been a psychotherapist, social worker, director of a community program for substance abuse prevention, and co-ordinator for health education grants for the city of Quincy, and she had worked on local women's issues. She knew the city very well over a couple of decades of work. She knew the art of com-munity organizing and she knew how to write grants. All of this would come in handy over the years to come!

When she talked to the UCC area minister, Mary Lou was told this church was at the "bottom of the bottom," the weakest con-gregation in the denominational region. So she decided to go into the interview with the call committee with a plan. The church had a couple years of money left and so they were ready to roll the wheel, call a pastor, and give it one grand shot. Or so they said. They had sold the parsonage to get the cash to pay a full-time pastor's salary for three years. They hired her and put all their bets on Mary Louise Gifford.

There was not a long line of folks behind her looking to go to Wollaston.

Even with an energized and gifted pastor coming in, the odds were stacked against Wollaston Church. If you were to take all the churches consisting of twenty aging worshipers in expensive build-ings with no significant money left, the vast majority will be gone within a few years. Few survive. Few muster the will to turn around. Mary Lou was wise enough to know this. She had basically two years to crank up the momentum; otherwise the third year would simply be winding things down in order to close. So she sought help from two well-respected coaches, who work with new church plants, and she proceeded to work with the urgency of a church planter. Almost all church planter pastors know that they have roughly two years for something to happen or they will be moving on to their next opportunity. She and the Wollaston Church pulled it off, with God's help.

Almost a decade later, they are thriving. And they demonstrate that even a church with a 98 percent chance of imminent demise can be saved. Just because most will not make the choices they need to make in no way keeps your church or mine from making those choices. Even though the established patterns, behaviors, and expectations are that the Wollaston churches will die, there is no reason to accept this as inevitable. Churches can *choose life*. Wollaston did.

But business as usual was not going to cut it for Wollaston. Business as usual meant an almost certain church closing. So here's what happened:

A small group of people had basically run the church for many years, controlling virtually everything. It had gotten bossy at times. Church closets were stuffed full of members' personal belongings. Continuation of business as usual would have soon run the church into the ground.

So one of Mary Lou's first moves was to initiate the suspension of the church bylaws, creating a little breathing room in order to create a new lead team. Few of the former leaders were asked to serve.

The church inherited an executive committee governing structure from days when it was much larger. By 2003, the executive committee was as big as the worship attendance. They knocked it down to a church council of six people. They looked for two long-term members, two medium-tenure members, and two who had been around less than five years. It was a good move, greatly speeding up decision-making at a point when the church needed to move quickly. These six met twice a month for two years.

About the same time, they discontinued their struggling choir and introduced PowerPoint in worship, shooting hymn lyrics on the wall. If the governance structures had not shaken some of the change-resistant folks out of the tree, the worship changes surely did. These changes and this tough approach up-front caused quite a bit of furor, cooking the two dozen attendees down to fourteen within a few months.

They rocked along with a dozen or so in worship for a time, and then they added one or two, and then another. By the time the worship attendance had grown back to twenty, Mary Lou made the very unconventional move to make Wollaston a teaching parish. She took the field supervision course at the seminary, brought a seminarian in for a yearlong stint (a pastoral intern), shared the preaching, and freed up some time. This freed-up time enabled Mary Lou to do two things she knew well how to do—write grants and deal as a therapist with the "wreckage of the past" with the tiny cadre of folks who were committed to this church.

Nine seminarians *and more than $400,000 in grants* later, the church sees now that they have something to offer, not only to their community, but also to those who serve with them. Becoming a teaching parish lifted their self-esteem. Lately, the church has begun taking graduates in their first assignment post-seminary, a position of pastoral resident. The pastoral residents train at Wollaston in the strategies of church turnaround, and then they go on to serve a church that is in the same shape as Wollaston was back in 2003.

Mary Lou describes her feelings just walking through the church building in her first year: "As I walked around the church building, I saw physical plant issues everywhere. I saw holes in the walls, paint peeling, walls caving in, closets stuffed with papers and other remnants of the past. Water came into the building every time it rained. . . . The building smelled of mildew all year long" (p. 22, *The Turnaround Church*).

Slowly and steadily, even as the church was reborn, these issues had to be addressed. Children's rooms had to be painted. Water issues had to be fixed. And it could not happen overnight. They just didn't have that kind of cash. The old-timers were used to the disrepair. Newcomers were appalled.

Getting the church on the National Historic Registry produced $30,000 for the most urgent building repairs. That means the church was able to spend $30,000 on operating expense, that otherwise might have been diverted at a critical moment when the church needed to think short-term and jumpstart ministry.

Amazingly, almost all of the folks who were on board when they launched the teaching parish ministry are still around years later! This lack of turnover among the core, once a unity of purpose was found, has brought the stability to make possible much of what the church has done in the last few years.

What exactly did they do? They went extraverted to the community! They began to offer programs, often funded in part by grants that they found, and shaped by the nature of the grant and attentiveness to the needs and interests of the community.

The denomination recommended that they focus on a broader group of neighbors than young families—due in part to the need to build financial stability and the fact that young families rarely come with a ton of cash. They pondered this, and chose to focus first on young families with children anyway. They looked at their local demographics and judged that this would be a group that they could effectively reach. As a result, they are a younger church today than they might otherwise be. And they are still struggling financially.

They began Family Fun Nights, one Friday every few months. Mary Lou recalls imagining the possibilities for this when she first saw the stage in the parish hall, built in a day when the church had energy for various performances. With Family Fun Nights, however, the stage would be used in a way different from the way most churches think about such facility resources. It would be used to serve and gather the community, not to entertain the church folks. Family Fun Nights would be an event totally "for them" as opposed to "for us," events designed for and with neighborhood families with young children. One night it might be a movie and popcorn, the next it might be a marionette troupe—in all cases they worked to get the word out and to frame this as a community-building event, not a church-recruitment event. More recently, the fun nights have morphed into Block Parties.

The church launched a summer program for children called Healthy Kids Vacation Camp. They funded it through state grants for children's health education and addiction prevention. The focus of the camp was not religious but was in line with community needs, and it helped the church build a partnership with several area families. They advertised via local schools and the constituents that they had found with the Family Fun Nights. Because of the public service nature of the camp, they even qualified for free ads on local cable TV. After the first camp, two families from Healthy Kids Vacation Camp began to attend on Sundays. The church then realized that they needed to upgrade their Sunday morning ministry in order to bring the same quality to their faith education programs as they offered in the community programs. Only then could they offer Sunday morning as a credible next step in terms of people's involvement with the church.

So they found a grant to help them hire a director for Sunday morning children's ministry, just a few hours a week. They were still a very small congregation, and most of their folks worked full-time. Getting a strong Sunday morning children's leader helped them quickly pull the quality of the Sunday morning experience to the level they desired.

A few patterns should be noted:

- Grants provided start-up funds for a lot of what Wollaston has tried, something that has not been a major theme in any of the previous stories.

- The prime measure of success is the number of outsiders coming in.

- Volunteers run the outreach initiatives.

- Most of the new initiatives run about a three-year life span, and then the volunteers and/or participants get tired, and they give it a break.

- The energy freed from letting go of one program enables the start of another. (This is a pattern that I noted in several of the congregations I studied for this book. While it might seem like defeat to let a successful program rest, this actually keeps the church from getting stuck.)

One of the persons who joined the church in recent years is Fran. She lives directly across the street. Fran began to notice more activity, more people coming and going, and younger people mixed in with the older. She began attending a garden club that met in the church building. There she met Mary Lou. Mary Lou invited her back, saying she needed her help. It is hard to remember exact words, but Fran remembers the invitation to help, not an invitation to come and sit in a pew. Fran's first response to that invitation was on a snowy morning when the church had scheduled a Christmas fair. Fran looked out her front window early that morning and re-alized someone would have to shovel snow for folks to get in for the fair. So she grabbed a shovel and went to clear snow. She met folks coming in as she shoveled, and she hung around. From that entry point into the church community, Fran never left. I share her story because it represents the stories of thousands of people whose first foray into a church community is through volunteering or helping with some community-oriented event or service rather than coming to worship.

After the first two years, as activity increased, the six people on the lead team who met every two weeks began to get tired. It was more than they could handle. In the early days of the turnaround, a simple structure was good for quick decision-making. But in year three they sensed a need to make a shift. So they called the church into a retreat for a conversation about ministry and leadership. They shifted the group of six into a group of stewards, who work in a team-partnership with several other groups of folks.

After the third year, the church was growing, and there was money left to pay the pastor and extend another year and then another after that. In addition, and with concerted effort to secure funding with outside partners, they have been able to add the pas-toral resident position and a part-time music leader/administrator.

At Christmas Eve 2006, Peter Johnson came to sub on the organ. He was, at the time, administrator of a larger church in Boston. Wollaston needed help with music, and with publications and social media. They also needed someone to unlock the door for activities and groups, and to interface with them on behalf of the church. Peter came on staff part-time in 2007 to do a mix of these tasks—all areas where he is gifted. In addition, he writes grants. In fact, Peter points out, that all staff persons at Wollaston are expected to write grants.

Prior to Peter's coming, members of the church assisted Mary Lou in securing a grant for $20,000 from the Calvin Institute, a grant for worship renewal. This made it possible to bring in top-notch speakers and artists across a year's time to a group of local churches. One of these speakers was Thomas Long, author of *Beyond the Worship Wars: Building Vital and Faithful Worship* (Alban, 2001). Tom Long opened the congregation up to possibilities about how they could develop greater artfulness of their worship. It was on Peter's first full weekend working at Wollaston, that he had the pleasure of escorting Dr. Long back and forth from the hotel, and learning a great deal about congregational singing.

In 2009, Mary Lou published *The Turnaround Church*, drawing significantly from the experience of the Wollaston rebirth. Tom Long wrote the foreword. The book relies heavily on interviews with ten of the folks who have made this journey with her. If the Wollaston story piques your interest or seems particularly relevant to your church, you can learn more directly from Mary Lou there.

Today, Wollaston Church gathers between seventy-five to ninety folks in worship most weeks. Young children abound. The church pulled off a Christmas cantata in 2010 for the first time in nearly thirty years, drawing together a seasonal choir of twenty people, most of whom did not read music. They treated it as worship rather than performance. They built sets. They sewed costumes. Lots of folks pitched in. The church was packed, and they report "not a dry eye in the house."

During the summer of 2011, in order to keep the place alive during the brief and glorious Boston summer, they chose to just give their folks the whole weekend for personal time, and they shifted weekly summer worship to Wednesday nights.

Few churches are gutsy enough or creative enough to simply move their services to midweek in the summer to keep things fresh. Wollaston has become that kind of place . . . there may be a little tinge of old-church smell in the air every now and then, but rarely will you find a fresher, more nimble community of faith!

Given the steady demographic changes occurring around them, nimble is a good thing. While many of their Asian neighbors have attended various community activities in their building, they have yet to add many Chinese folks into the worship life of the congregation. Mary Lou notes that most churches in the community tend to be racially and culturally homogeneous. Nevertheless, given the projected growth of the Chinese community, this demographic shift will eventually affect the way the church staffs its programs and the way it does just about everything.

Just as the present looks and feels a bit different than the past, it is a good bet that the future at Wollaston UCC will look and feel considerably different than the present.

Stay tuned!

POSTCARDS FROM WOLLASTON

- Its worth all the hard work!
- Be realistic. Define what's important to you. Set goals. Commit to move toward those goals one day at a time.
- The primary purpose of gathering is to worship God. Focusing on worship has done wonders for us.
- Use the gifts God gives you!
- Believe and work together and you can make a difference.
- We truly feel God working in and through each one of us.

6

THE GREAT COMMISSION CHURCH

First United Methodist, Sikeston, Missouri

Sikeston is a county seat town in what they call the boot heel of Missouri, in the far southeastern corner of the state, not far from the Mississippi River, and close enough to Memphis to feel like the Old South. Racial and economic divides are pretty sharp here, with some of the wealthiest and some of the poorest folks in Missouri among its sixteen thousand people. A few decades back, there were more millionaires per capita here than anywhere else in Missouri. Quite a few families today share in second- or third-generation wealth passed down from those days.

First United Methodist Church has long been one of the places in Sikeston where the old money folks gathered. The church was friendly, in the southern sense of the word: good manners to your face and deep suspicions behind your back if you were new or out to rock the boat. This was a church that took its traditions seriously, existing to keep long-time members happy and to change as little as possible. The pastor's job traditionally here was to show up for everything that went on, say a prayer to get things started, and sometimes another prayer to send folks home. The pastor was a personal chaplain for the dues-paying members, expected to give respect to the old guard, deliver succinct and inspirational sermons, and to follow members all the way to Memphis, if necessary, to visit them in the hospital.

Long-time members report a recurring pattern of intense power struggles in the church. They attribute this to the number of community leaders and major business owners in the church. These persons were used to calling the shots in every other arena of their lives, and so they brought these habits to church.

In 1968, when their downtown building burned, the church split over where and what to rebuild. A sizable contingent left the church because the new building was to be constructed on the growing edge of town and the architecture was to be modern. Things settled back to normalcy for about thirty years after that. And, of course, it was the pastor's job to mend any ill feelings.

Then in 2001 the church started a contemporary worship service. They called it Living Water Celebration. The same thing happened in Sikeston as happened in Holton, Kansas, when they added a similar service the very same year. A considerable number of folks opposed this move, and a rift appeared in the church.

Two years later when Tom Bandy visited the church as a consultant, his report spoke of "strong personalities" and "extreme pastor dependence," even to the point of addiction. One member, Jill, recalls the factions at the time of the Bandy visit: one group determined to keep everything as it was and another group hungry to go deeper in their spiritual journey than they felt they could go with traditional worship forms. When the latter group created the new service, the traditional folks took it as an insult, that their worship was not good enough. And if the point of life were to keep everything the same, with the corollary assumption that the old ways are the best ways, then a new style of worship service would be perceived as a major threat.

About the same time the new service started, the church built a multipurpose facility, with a gym. Sikeston normally paid off its construction projects fairly quickly, but, in this case, with attitudes a bit raw, a three-million-dollar mortgage hung around after building completion.

In 2005, Geoff Posegate was sent to First Church Sikeston as pastor. Geoff had just led a conflicted church in the Kansas City area through facility relocation. The bishop figured if he could pull that off, he could handle Sikeston.

Geoff read *The First Ninety Days* by Michael Watkins as he got started in his new post. He conducted numerous interviews and asked lots of questions in the summer of 2005. He then shared his impressions at a special dinner for church leaders. The dinner gathering was helpful in that it quickly shook folks out of the bushes who resonated with his vision. It also enabled Geoff to clearly signal that he had not come to "keep shop" but "to align this church with the Great Commission." He focused his early energy on developing leaders, leaders to handle conflict in the youth department, leaders to help the church pay off its building debt, leaders in worship, and so on.

One day, a prominent member of the church came by Geoff's office, irate, perhaps speaking on behalf of several other unhappy people. The man believed that Geoff was spending too much time focusing the church on reaching others and not being friendly enough to those who belong to the church. This man wanted Geoff to schmooze the old money, stop rocking the boat, and get folks in a good mood, so that the debt would naturally get paid off.

But Geoff did not budge off vision. Slowly, new (and old) leaders were developed. The church increased its emphasis on mission beyond itself, illustrated by its response to a local ice storm in the winter of 2007–08.

But attendance in worship did not budge either, hanging at just over three hundred a Sunday all through this time. This is larger than any other church in this book prior to transformation.

The church was locked in a stalemate between two factions, and chances were good that the conflict would reassert itself the day that Geoff left. Simply by the force of Geoff's personality, he was essentially forcing a truce. But unless something deeper changed, it would be a temporary truce. In a small town, the preachers come and they go, but some realities persist across many decades.

This might have been the end of this story, but for a helpful intervention from a denominational leader! (Occasionally, they *can* be helpful.)

Enter Bob Farr. Bob Farr is the director of Congregational Transformation for the Missouri Annual Conference of the United Methodist Church. In his first career, Bob was a cop. If he had been born a few generations earlier in these parts, he could have been Rooster Cogburn. I do not believe I am exaggerating. Bob Farr is an extremely no-nonsense kind of guy.

Bob works for another guy named Bob: United Methodist bishop Robert Schnase (pronounced SHNAY-zee), author of the bestselling book *Five Practices of Faithful Congregations.* In recent years, the two Bobs explored how they might lead scores of Missouri United Methodist congregations to new life. Not just one here and one there, while most continued to sink—but to truly turn around their denominational region.

They knew of only one person who had ever turned around a major region of an old American denomination—and that was Paul Borden, formerly the executive director of American Baptist Churches of the West (northern California and Nevada). In the 1990s Paul designed an intervention strategy whereby a good portion of the ABC congregations on the west coast came to life again—so many that the region itself reversed its long membership decline and grew by 30 percent in only a few years. The two Bobs adapted many of the principles of that experience to their context. Bob Farr says, "We Methodized Borden." The result was a program for transformation in Missouri United Methodist congregations. They called it the Healthy Church Initiative.

In short, the Healthy Church Initiative works like this:

1. The governing body of the congregation votes to enter HCI.

2. A designated team in the congregation begins praying regularly and methodically for the church's ministry.

3. The pastor agrees to participate in an ongoing group of pastors, working with a mentor, who are reading and learning together about strategies and practices of leading dynamic congregations.

4. The congregation sends a group of its lay leaders to two training events that align with what the pastors are reading in their group.

5. A team of two consultants (trained by the judicatory) comes in for a weekend consultation with the congregation. They end the consultation with a report that includes five commendations, five concerns, and five recommendations for action.

6. The congregation has a month or so to chew on the recommendations; then the governing body votes on the recommendations as a set. Up or down.

7. Once they vote the recommendations in, they proceed to make changes in line with what the church has voted to do. (If they vote down the recommendations, it's game over; and the denomination sends its resource people someplace else.)

8. If they vote to proceed, then a coach works with the pastor and leaders for about eighteen months to hold them accountable to what they have voted to do.

In the case of Sikeston, the program was sold on the premise that "we pay all this money to the denomination, and here is a chance to get top level consultation for a meager fee, and thus to get something for our money." They demanded a live meeting with Bob Farr before they would agree to enter the program. When Bob came out for the question and answer meeting about the program, he set the ground rules:

- Bob was willing to stay all night until people got their questions answered.

- Each person got one question, and that was it, until everyone had a chance to ask, and then people could ask a second question.

The meeting went for four hours; but after an evening of posturing, occasional huffing and territorial "peeing on fire hydrants," the proposal to enter HCI passed overwhelmingly.

The church established their prayer team. A group of twenty or so leaders began reading together over the summer. Half of these leaders stayed together through the fall to keep reading, praying, and thinking together. Two books that they found especially meaningful are Paul Borden's *Direct Hit* and Henry Blackaby's *Experiencing God.* They also gathered data on the church and community and made preparations for a consultation with Bob Farr in February 2009.

Bob and a district superintendent from another part of Missouri formed the consultation team. (The district superintendent, Bart Hildreth, would stay with them as a coach for longer than eighteen months.) Bob and Bart spent two days in Sikeston, attending worship, looking around at classes and groups, conducting on-site interviews, meeting with the staff, and so forth. At the end of the time, they gave their report and rode off into the sunset like Kansas gun slingers, leaving the Sikeston folks with forty days to process what had just happened. After that there would be a churchwide vote on the whole package, without amendments.

It was a tense month. The report generated controversy around several recommended changes. One recommendation, however, especially galled some of the old guard. The consultants found Geoff to be exhausted after four years of trying to lead this operation. They recommended a two-month sabbatical. (Given the firestorm that he would live through during the early months of implementation, this became especially helpful.)

Sally, the church council chair, led several town hall gatherings during this month, allowing folks to ask questions and share feelings about the recommendations. They recall one particular meeting as a real "barn burner." People were angry and they came to vent. (In fact, this phenomenon is common with churches that pursue HCI; Geoff feels that it is a very helpful part of the journey—to just let people vent their feelings.)

Sally stayed cool and said to the crowd assembled, "It's all right. It's all right to express where you are, to express your feelings. That is what we are here to do." The turning point in the meeting came when a long-time member who sings in the Chancel Choir took the mike. She said, "I do not want to see our church die. These are things we must do so that we don't die, even if we don't agree with everything." In most church transformation stories there are pivotal moments when the momentum clearly turns—some feel that this became such a moment in Sikeston.

The big vote came on Palm Sunday. More than two hundred people stayed after worship for the meeting—the largest congregational meeting in recent memory. The forces against the proposal had organized. As is typical of such meetings in old churches, people came to the meeting who had not been around in years. The vote went two to one in favor of accepting the report and adopting all recommendations. There was some relief, that after such organized opposition, the vote expressed a clear mandate. Some husbands and wives, as well as parents and their adult children, cancelled out each other's vote. Though feelings ran deep, these families all knew finally that unity and compromise would be more crucial than winning this vote.

In the months that followed, at every point when tough decisions were required, this vote gave the church's leaders the courage to keep moving forward. If First Church had backed down from this moment in order to forge greater consensus, they would have certainly squandered their greatest moment of opportunity in this generation.

The consultants cited the following strengths in the church:

- A highly skilled pastor
- Resources—both people and finances
- Great location with high visibility
- Solid building with lots of space—well maintained except for the children's wing

- Crisis response in the community

Their five concerns were as follows:

- The Great Commission, cited as central in their mission statement, is not being implemented effectively. Their dollars and energy are producing a "poor harvest."
- Administrative structures (staff and lay committees) are not well formed for the purpose of making disciples of Jesus.
- Children's space is not well maintained.
- The worship services are competing with each other rather than complementing each other; as a result there is division within and a poor witness in the community.
- Antiquated and inadequate forms of communication

The five recommendations related to:

- Mission
- Ministry structure
- Church facility
- Worship
- Communication

With regard to mission: a new mission statement would be written and approved by church council by Easter 2009, one week after the vote. Their new statement became "Leading people in new life with Jesus." They obviously had to work on this during the crazy month between the consultation and the vote—which in itself was a helpful exercise as they pondered their church's future.

In May, the pastor would call the staff, the church council and the congregation to a weekend of prayer. This event would be facilitated by an outsider with a two-fold purpose: (1) confession for failure in marshalling their resources to share their church and faith effectively with their neighbors and (2) prayer for God to "open their hearts" with compassion for their neighbors and a vision for reaching them and leading them to a faith relationship with Christ.

By September, another outside facilitator would lead a church-wide event called an Envisioning Day. The pastor would then write a new vision statement for the church within two weeks. From this process, Geoff proposed the following vision statement and vehicles toward the vision:

> First United Methodist Church will fulfill our mission of **leading people in new life with Jesus** by building relationships with *unreached* people, *post-church* people, and *too-much-church* people for the purpose of making disciples for Jesus Christ."
>
> The primary vehicles for this relationship building will be:

- CONNECTING EVENTS (comedy theaters, guest musicians and leaders, Christmas Eve off-site, etc.)
- A CONNECTIONS MINISTRY (more than 180 people and ten new, trained small-group leaders in an all-church, small-group effort)
- A DISCIPLESHIP PATHWAY (which will be explained under Ministry Structure)
- OUR SIGNATURE MISSION(S) (mentor support for high school athletic teams, reading ministry to under-resourced preschoolers)
- EXPECTANT WORSHIP (which will be explained under Worship)

Finally, the recommendation on mission directed the pastor and staff to lead an audit of the church's ministries, assessing everything they did and every dollar they spent. They were then instructed to make recommendations for changes to better align the church's behavior with its stated priorities. This was to all to be completed, approved, and implemented by February 1, 2010. In the end, no ministry was discontinued. But several ministries were moved to the margins, no longer supported by staff time or finances.

With regard to organizational structure, the pastor would work with his coach to recommend a reorganization of the church's staffing strategy in line with the church's mission and vision. The staff parish relations committee would work to implement this new structure by midyear 2010. This report resulted in a discontinuance of the associate pastor position (which was filled with a talented leader at the time) and the addition of four coordinators who report directly to the pastor. The new coordinators would be in charge of worship, faith growth, administration, and mission. All other staff would relate to these four departments, with everyone responsible to set goals for new persons reached, leaders developed, and percentage of growth in their areas.

The faith growth coordinator now manages a process of developing people as disciples of Jesus that flows as follows:

- Group lunch with the pastor (orientation to the church's mission, Q & A, and distribution of inventories for assessment of spiritual gifts and personality profile)

- One-on-one meeting with the faith growth coordinator (placement in small group & choosing ministry involvement)

- Two years of intentional learning in a group context (in trimesters, beginning with basic beliefs and spiritual disciplines, followed by a year-long study through the Bible, followed by a course on "fruit of the Spirit," followed by varied electives)

Soon all new members will join the church with the expectation that they will participate in the faith growth journey as outlined above. This will probably mean fewer new members in the immediate future—and could ultimately function to invert the relationship between membership and attendance. Instead of a thousand members and three hundred who show up for worship, this church could instead wind up with three hundred members and a thousand who show up for worship.

Meanwhile the five major chairpersons of committees (in the old structure) were tasked to "evaluate the lay governance structures of First Church in order to create and shape a pastor-led, streamlined, accountable leadership model of governance which supports the mission of the church." They were given the latter half of 2009 to accomplish this. By January 2010, the church implemented a new structure, with a small church council of fifteen persons meeting once every other month, working essentially as a board of directors, with the pastor leading in an executive capacity, accountable to them. (In 2012, they further reduced the size of the church council to nine persons.)

Regarding the facilities, the director of children's ministries led a team to visit five churches known for excellence in ministry to children. The recommendation stipulated that at least $30,000 be allocated toward upgrades in the children's space, with work to be completed by spring 2010. The work was paid in full by special donations. The vision of a vibrant children's ministry energized the donors. Another similar recommendation stipulated at least $20,000 for renovation of teen ministry space. It was also recommended that the church improve its signage. Special donations paid for these improvements in full.

Regarding worship, the church leaders did not balk from making big changes, combining the two traditional services into one hour at 9 AM (including the traditional service with choir that had been held at 11 AM for generations), and moving the Living Water service to the prime 11 AM slot. When they asked what schedule best suited their mission to the community, this was a very clear and easy decision. They moved to develop a stronger children's ministry at both the 10 AM hour and concurrent with the Living Water service. (The consultants did not tell them exactly what to do with worship times—they left it to local leaders to wrestle the details, giving more integrity and credibility to these tough decisions when they were made.)

The worship changes resulted in a sharp loss of attendance in 2009, down to about 260 a week in the fall of that year. However, by winter 2010, the Living Water service began to grow and, soon after, to explode with people. Eventually the name Living Water was replaced with Journey. The service grew rapidly through 2010 and was up another 37 percent in early 2011 over the 2010 levels. More recently, they added a Saturday evening version of the Journey service with about fifty-six people attending in the first months.

In terms of communication, the print newsletter and website were overhauled and an e-newsletter added. The church web address is now www.thefunchurch.org. Some folks thought this sounded frivolous, but the name was created for a public who believed that church (especially this one) was boring, stuffy, or possibly a country club church. They wanted to turn that perception on its head. This also underlined the fact that, they had *chosen fun*—even though the choice itself was not a lot of fun for leaders for the first several months!

In late 2009, while all this good work was occurring on multiple fronts, worship attendance dropped to the lowest level in memory. Quite a bit of donor money had by now also walked out the door. Many were convinced that all this change was taking their church down the toilet. The pastor came under relentless attack from the old guard who had lost the vote and whose power was eroding by the week with the new structures. Geoff remembers this as a season of fast changes and bitter complaining, "hell on wheels" in his words. Geoff worked with a therapist to care for himself even as he worked with the coach to keep the changes moving at church.

"How could we turn our church over to the opinions of someone from the outside?" "This is all too heavy-handed!" "We have thrown the people who pay the bills around here out of the sanctuary at 11 AM and relegated them to a second-rate time slot!" "How are people we haven't even met yet more important than those who have been a part of our church family for years?" "I have never seen attendance so low or feelings so hurt." "Just look at what you have done to our church!" And so it went, all through the fall of 2009.

Yet, in the midst of this, several folks describe a change that happened in meetings that fall and in the way that decisions were made. Every decision started in prayer. Every conversation oriented itself with the Great Commission as a compass. Leaders began to consciously shift their dependence away from the big donors (who historically had bailed things out) toward God, trusting that somehow, if they made decisions that honored God, God would take care of finances.

I take you through all of these details because I do not believe that First UMC could have made the enormous gains that they made in 2010–11 without having lived through the intensity, the pain, and the comprehensiveness of change that occurred in 2009.

By Advent 2009, the tension began to ease. One of the church's discoveries in all of this was that they excelled at special events and parties, so they planned several quality events for the Advent/Christmas season, including a fun night with a comedian and a couple great music events. The associate pastor, whose position was ending as a position for appointed clergy, was assigned as the interim coordinator of worship. He proved to be gifted at the task, really helping worship life to move forward and to sparkle in early 2010. The worship team began to rethink worship each week as a special stand-alone event, unlike any other. Fifty-two special events each year! This helped them play to their gifts.

In mid-2010, the church hired Brad Aycock as the worship coordinator. As an adult convert to the faith, Brad totally understood what it would mean for worship at Sikeston First to connect with people who lived outside church culture or who had burned out on it.

In early 2010, worship attendance began to grow. By Easter, the church had gained back all the numbers lost (with mostly new people), and by fall 2010, they were exploding. Within two years of the legendary Palm Sunday showdown, First UMC had surged by more than 30 percent in attendance above where they started— a burst of growth almost unheard of in such a staid and aristocratic southern church. Not only had worship attendance soared, but participation levels for children and youth had doubled. A woman in the church died and left $100,000 for "anything but buildings"—helping to cover the startup costs for additional staff positions. By 2011, half the adults on Sunday were active in a small group. Financial giving spiked upward. The church moved ahead of schedule on its debt service. Volunteers and leaders were multiplying, enabling more ministry expansion. Scores of new families were flowing into the church.

The transformation had been breathtaking.

All this was possible, in large part, because a theological consensus about the value of inviting others to faith in Christ already existed among many of the people at First UMC. Geoff worked steadily to strengthen this consensus his first three years as pastor here. Yet their church practices and structures were not aligned to their basic theology.

Not every church can draw upon this kind of consensus, but many churches in conservative communities can. When I used to work as a judicatory-based church consultant in the southern United States, I discovered that whenever we lifted up the Great Commission in the life of a congregation, we often created amazing leverage for change—drawing on the power of latent theological assumptions in so many heartland congregations.

First Church Sikeston is a case where the church simply realigned itself to its deepest values, values rooted in a heritage of camp meetings and altar calls in days past. In Sikeston, when the issue was pressed and brought into the light, the value of "leading people to salvation through Jesus Christ" was more powerful than the value of preserving a clubby social network. Finally, these people were willing to rock the boat in order to be faithful to God and neighbors.

POSTCARDS FROM SIKESTON

- Don't give up!
- Wrap yourself in prayer. And God will do a new thing!
- Vision what you imagine God wants it to look like without the barriers. Then talk about it. Pray about it!
- Don't be afraid to vision a future totally impossible without God!

- This church is not my pastor's boss. And this church is not God. We are to follow God, as is our pastor.

- Pray and let God show you.

- Make sure people know that they are not being left behind. Gather them back up! There will be plenty of emotions, but be sure everyone still knows that they are a part of the family (1 Samuel 30:18-19).

- I am an example of what change in a church will do. If you get down to what it's about: I am it. Change in the right way and people like me will walk in the door. Can I send myself on a post card? (New young adult member)

7

THE LET'S ROLL UP OUR SLEEVES CHURCH

Lake Alfred Presbyterian, Lake Alfred, Florida

Lake Alfred is a city of five thousand people surrounded by half a dozen small lakes, within a larger web of communities south of Orlando amid a larger array of lakes. It is a place with a decidedly slow pace and a village-like feel. When the summer humidity kicks in, you want to just sit down in the shade with a mint julep.

The locals remind me that there are four Walmarts within ten miles. So, there are lots of people around. About one out of four persons is older than sixty-five.

In the mid-twentieth century, when snowbirds and retirees were pouring into Central Florida from points north, Lake Alfred Presbyterian Church and countless others popped up. Florida was growing in all population segments during those years, but the growth rate was higher among senior citizens. Furthermore, seniors are more inclined to attend church than younger residents. So many of Florida's churches took on a decidedly senior personality during those years, even in communities that were not specifically designed for retirees. Then into the new century, the Boomers started to retire, and they arrived in Florida with somewhat different church habits and behaviors than those who came before them. Fewer of them came looking for a new church; more of them came looking simply for bridge groups and a golf course, possibly for a cardiologist.

Now, if the average age of new members in a church is sixty-four, and the church experiences a drop in people joining, then it will not be many years before the church itself will begin to decline. For the average sixty-four-year-old, it will only be around fifteen to twenty years before his or her pew will go empty. A younger church might rock along for two or three decades after the rate of new members drops before people begin to take notice, and the median age begins to notably rise. In Florida, it typically takes only a few years before you notice. Because of this, some of the churches and judicatory regions in the Sunshine State that may have won accolades for growth in the 1980s are now slipping precipitously.

Lake Alfred Presbyterian is one such church that almost ran out of steam. The church is a century old. Though they have always been affiliated with some Presbyterian group, they have a history of thinking and acting somewhat independently of any denominational tribe. They have never been a large church, and they have a historical pattern of declining and rebounding across the years. Four times they have received substantial financial gifts, only to see those funds slowly spent down on operating expenses.

Their pastor, Roland Castro, estimates that in 2008 Lake Alfred Presbyterian came within six months of running out of cash and energy to continue. This is the story of how they came back, with the loving leadership of a pastor who was already in his second decade with them and a regional judicatory leader who made it her number one job to resource her churches for the twenty-first century. This is the only church turnaround story in this book where the key events happened on the watch of a long-tenure pastor in his second decade at the church.

Roland came to Lake Alfred in 1993. He came bursting with energy, such as one would expect from a former new church planter. During his first service of communion there, however, when he slightly deviated from the liturgy, he learned that folks at Lake Alfred did not take kindly to change.

For Roland's first ten years here, he tried to get the congregation at Lake Alfred to grow, to try new, to dream. He pushed, and folks would resist, or they would smile to his face and then just keep on about life as normal. At one point, they wrote a vision statement a mile long (that said essentially nothing). They read *The Purpose Driven Church* together, and found it no more helpful than the vision statement project. They even read a little book called *I Refuse to Lead a Dying Church.*

Many of the Presbyterians in Lake Alfred had come to Florida to end their lives well: working less, playing more, and tending mostly to inward concerns. They were out neither to change the world or to change their church at this point. Gladys, a Lake Alfred member, would characterize her church as "lethargic" for most of the time she has been around. In her words, the attitude was, "Come to church if you don't have anything better going on!"

Like many declining churches, Lake Alfred had overorganized themselves into seventeen committees (for fifty people in worship), and yet still they could not get anyone to do anything, nor could they get many decisions made. The Session (the top local church administrative body for Presbyterians) too often re-decided whatever the other committees decided. The only ministry teams that could choose to do something without major deliberation and committee action were the choir and property management team. Roland says, "Everything else was hog-tied."

Roland was getting nowhere leading these people, and, understandably, he was thinking about leaving.

Then in the summer of 2005 a series of four hurricanes moved through the community. Like many Florida churches that year, Lake Alfred had to leave its damaged sanctuary and worship somewhere else. They spent eighteen months worshiping in the fellowship hall, around tables. Before the hurricanes, people described the energy in the sanctuary as really low. Once forced into the fellowship hall for worship, people really began to interact with each other—to act like community in the context of worship. They also began to talk about God-moments and to talk about spiritual issues again, for the first time in many years. And the church began to grow a little. The crisis of the hurricane became an opportunity for some good changes to begin. Beyond worship, however, it was still like "pulling teeth" to get anyone at Lake Alfred to do much.

In 2007, the women elders of the Session invited other women in the church into an initiative they called Presbyterian Women in Action. They were not affiliated with any national organization—they made it all up as they went. The sole purpose of this new group was to brainstorm ways to help the church to raise funds. Over the next year, these women cooked up and ran several creative and successful fund-raisers that helped to shrink the financial bleed. Thanks to them, in 2008 the church was still in the red, but still in business, and much closer to solvency. *These women bought the church time, and without them, there would be no Lake Alfred Presbyterian Church today!*

Enter Mary McKee. Mary is on the staff of the Tampa Bay Presbytery of the Presbyterian Church in the USA. The presbytery executive, Gerry Tyer, and his staff created a program for this presbytery called the REACH Initiative. It bears marked similarity to the Healthy Church Initiative that Missouri United Methodists developed. As in Missouri, it is based on the work of Paul Borden. Mary became the primary staff person from the presbytery, assigned to work with Lake Alfred Church.

As an early part of the REACH Initiative, several groups from various Tampa Bay Presbyterian churches came to an event in 2008 in which I taught the six choices from my book *I Refuse to Lead a Dying Church.* That meeting is where I first ran across some of the folks from Lake Alfred, a group of women and Pastor Roland Castro. Following that gathering, several of the Presbyterian Women in Action, freshly energized by their success raising money, came back determined that they could help their church choose life—they could do more than simply raise funds. They added a Bible study and devotional component to their meetings.

From their original fund-raisers, they began to think in terms of serving the church, and then the community. They began to cook meals for the local Chamber of Commerce, then for the Gideons. Before long, thirty-six women were involved. They reached first for women within the church, and then they reached beyond. From cooking and baking, they expanded to creating a community food pantry. The focus of their work gradually shifted from fund-raising to serving others.

But they feel the turning point was when they decided to do *something*. They chose *now*. That was the critical choice. Once they started doing something, they began to see community needs, and they continued to move toward those needs. From the food ministry, they expanded to providing school uniforms for low-income children, providing soap for the school restrooms, and so on. With the women setting the pace, several men in the church also started a service group. As people came together to do something, relationships were strengthened as well. One thing strengthened another thing, and led to the next thing.

In the first year after they began the REACH initiative, the church leapt forward, approaching eighty in average worship attendance. Twenty-seven people joined the church in 2009, a big deal for a church this size!

Note the critical difference here between how a smaller church renews, compared to the much larger Sikeston church with almost ten times as many people. Both churches would use a similar consulting process. But in Lake Alfred, prior to the consultation, laity took the lead to start making things happen. The pastor had tried for ten years, but until laity took the lead, there was little progress. In Sikeston, the pastor had much more leverage.

In the context of this subtle but critical shift in lay initiative, with worship attendance rising, the church was ready for a consultation with Mary McKee in early 2008. Attitudes and energy were up, but the church was still organized for another time and place. It was still on its way to closing if there was not further positive change. After surveys and interviews, Mary made her report to the church in the context of a Sunday morning service the week after Easter.

She cited the following five strengths in the church:

- The church has a history of resilience.
- People in the church deeply treasure the relationships they find here.
- There is a higher than usual (for Presbyterians) interest in spiritual things and in spiritual growth.
- The church has a history of strong music, and they still value music highly in its life.
- The Presbyterian Women in Action have given the church a renewed sense of possibilities.

She cited the following five concerns:

- Members do not have a shared vision for the church.
- Too few people are trying to do too much work for this size church and this age of membership, and without sufficient training and organization.
- Members have significant anxiety about finances, in terms of (a) the shortage of money, (b) questions about accounting and management, and (c) communication about what's going on.
- The church has a batch of new members, but it is imperative that they be assimilated fully into church life, receiving their fresh ideas and their gifts.
- There are several silos of people in the church that need to be connected (so that there can be greater understanding and synergy).

And she gave them five prescriptions (the term deriving from the metaphor of the consultation as a check-up with a family physician), with the reminder that "under the REACH Covenant, a church must be willing to work on all five prescriptions."

- The church needs to develop a unifying sense of vision and a purpose that focuses decisions and actions.

- The Session reexamines all church programs in light of the above in order to reorganize/streamline the structure to fit the new vision/focus. This work should be completed in a retreat or Saturday meeting. (In other words, we are not to drag this out.)

- Recruit two persons from another PCUSA church with a financial background to (a) analyze finances of the church, (b) design a simple system of accounting and reporting, (c) recommend ways to cut costs, and (d) help the Session communicate all this to the congregation on an ongoing basis.

- With the help of the Presbytery, leadership will study how best to assimilate new members, design a plan for the church, and communicate that as fully as possible.

- The church will host a Saturday vision/connecting event to unify the silos and to invite all parties into the church's new plans.

The Session had until their next meeting to decide if they wished to continue REACH. To continue meant they would adopt the report and begin working wholeheartedly toward the five recommendations. They voted unanimously to adopt the report and proceed.

Within six weeks of the Session decision, they held a retreat in which they created a new vision statement for Lake Alfred Presbyterian Church. Mary told them it had to be "simple enough that they could fit it on a t-shirt." What they came up with may not be a statement ready for a megachurch. But it works for Lake Alfred. It's concise. You can organize around it. Their statement is "Moving together with Christ in . . . loving acceptance, growing faith, and reaching out."

Working from this vision, they nixed all seventeen committees and created seven teams:

- Worship
- Faith Growing

- Outreach

- Welcoming and Compassionate Care

- Property Management/Development

- Time and Talent Development

The Session then created clear expectations for all teams. Beyond these expectations, teams are given freedom to innovate, to follow the gifts and passions of their people, and have fun. Those expectations include these:

1. All meetings begin and end with prayer.

2. All goals of the teams must support the church vision statement.

3. All activities of the teams must comply with the *Book of Order* (PCUSA rule book).

4. All activities must stay within the bounds of the team's budget and blessing. (The blessing is the mandate given to a team, the realm of their responsibility.)

5. If a team runs out of funds, they must generate any additional needed funds.

6. Calendar dates are to be coordinated through the church secretary on a first come, first served basis.

7. Teams will work cooperatively when appropriate.

By creating boundaries, clear road rules, people know where the road shoulders are and where the road is headed. With a good highway, people feel more comfortable taking the initiative to travel on it, taking initiative without fear that they will be reprimanded for overstepping their authority or mandate. This is the ironic truth about clear boundaries documents—by telling us what we cannot do, they often help us get comfortable in the larger arena of what we can do. I have sometimes compared this to the United States economy—we need good infrastructure and clear laws so that we can feel secure in creating new businesses, inventing new systems, and dreaming as far as our imaginations can take us. This kind of system dynamic that balances permission with clear boundaries helps to build great churches in addition to great nations.

The new teams at Lake Alfred began to function on September 13, 2009, about fifteen months after their consultation. Information about what was happening was displayed prominently for several weeks prior to this. Members, elders, and others were encouraged to sign up for a team. Each team had to have at least one elder (Session member) on it, but that person could not chair the team. One does not have to be a church member to serve on a team.

Most folks jumped on a team. The level of member involvement kept going up. One member, Gail, says, "People started volunteering because they found areas in which they really felt they could be of service." Some teams create task groups for certain projects (a yard sale, a mission day, a church repair day, and other such events). They come and they go away, as needed. In this way, the church provides a place for sprinters to plug in, those persons who will volunteer in short-term bursts, but who will not or cannot commit to a long-term team.

Now, when the inevitable big-ticket maintenance issues arise related to the church building, the congregation is able to handle issues that would have closed their doors five years ago. With the increase in lay involvement in hands-on ministry projects, everything else has come along, including finances and a broader ownership of the church's occasional financial challenges. Improved accounting and reporting has further stabilized the finances.

Through all of this, Lake Alfred has remained a church of older adults. They have approached their decisions in ways that reflect their generational sensibilities. There are a few younger folks around and a handful of children with lots of spiritual grandparents. But Lake Alfred chose to be a better version of what it was rather than to attempt to become something they were not. Their focal audience is the retired golfer and empty-nester blue-collar worker.

Is it possible that such change could happen without some conflict? Not on your life. But the conflict was minimal in Lake Alfred, in large part because foundations were in place, laity took action, and momentum was positive going into the consultation.

The major push back came from a retired clergyperson (a snowbird) in the congregation who spent his summers up north and came back in winter 2009, after all the meetings, decisions, and changes had happened that summer. He was horrified at what he discovered and tried to tell people that the church could not do this, that it was not Presbyterian, and so forth. But at that point, the horse was out of the barn, so to speak. Several leaders had to say to him, forthrightly, that the church had made a decision and they were not going to back up on it. So he left for another congregation.

In all of this change, so deep into Roland's tenure at Lake Alfred, I figured that Roland must have grown as well. So I asked some of the people at Lake Alfred how their pastor had grown over the last four years as the church came back to life. I learned that Roland had always been a solid preacher and a caring pastor. But lately he moves with a new sense of energy, freedom, and confidence. He is more relaxed, "more led by the Word" in his preaching, less careful to tiptoe around and parse words, more comfortable just saying what he needs to say and giving space for folks who don't quite agree. In other words, his main growth was simply that he is now freer to be himself in the system.

The crisis of the hurricanes, the critical determination of a few women in the church, and the helpful intervention and coaching offered by a Presbytery staff member gave Roland a new church. All of this together gave him the church he had wanted all along, freed him up to have more fun, and saved him from having to go through the call process and move to another place in order to find it!

If you are a layperson ready to get off the pew and call your friends and neighbors into ministry action, Lake Alfred is a story of why you should waste no time! This is what can happen in your church, as the good things compound one on the other. If your talented pastor is tired of pushing against a brick wall, Lake Alfred is more relevant still. By all measures, Lake Alfred Presbyterian Church should have died by now. Scores of PCUSA churches that were healthier than they were in 1993 are now gone. Capable pastors and laity are present in so many churches. But they have not yet always found their synergy with one another.

Lake Alfred Presbyterian suggests that most churches closing this year could have avoided that outcome. But, please, please, take note that they needed a third party at Lake Alfred—a trusted friend, consultant, and advisor to help them make the necessary changes to move fully into a new chapter of their life.

POSTCARDS FROM LAKE ALFRED

- Bloom where you are planted.
- Don't give up the ship!
- God's arms are not too short.
- Faith and good works go together.
- We learned we could not do it all. Put trying to do it all aside and act on your strengths.
- We are a church of seniors—*and there is nothing wrong with it!*
- In all things, God works for good for those who love God and are called according to God's purpose. (the Apostle Paul)

8

THE PROGRESSIVE ALTERNATIVE CHURCH

Irvine United Congregational, Irvine, California

Orange County, California, brings many things to mind. Disneyland. The Crystal Cathedral. Conservative politics. Good beaches. Pete Seeger's song "Little Boxes." For me, growing up in Southern California (and apparently for the creators of the sitcom *Weeds*), that song described perfectly what the subdivisions looked like from the freeway en route to Disneyland and the beach. In the sixties and seventies, Orange County was quintessential twentieth-century suburbia: mostly white residents on the outskirts of a large metropolitan area, living in thousands of tidy homogeneous dwellings, near freeways that could carry Daddy to work in the big city beyond.

More recently, the OC (as it is sometimes called) has become a much more diverse and, arguably, more interesting place. The white population now makes up less than half of the county and is steadily diminishing. In Irvine, Mayor Sukhee Kang is the first Korean-American mayor of a major U.S. city. He claims that thirty-five different languages are spoken in his city.

As one might expect in such circumstances, many of the mainline Protestant churches have fallen on hard times. Some of these were neighborhood churches built on three-acre lots, never very large to begin with. Even the Crystal Cathedral, however, teeters near bankruptcy. These churches have aged rapidly, especially with (1) fast changing worship tastes among those who are interested in church, (2) even faster changing ethnic population patterns, and (3) the considerable exodus of persons with liberal social values from organized religion. Some of the latter are children of Christian parents, and quite a few now see organized religion as a problem and an instigator for social injustice.

The percentage of Orange County voters identifying as Republican has dropped below 50 percent in recent years. Nonetheless, many of the newer groups are socially conservative. And some of the remaining white enclaves are radically conservative, living almost in a fortress mentality with respect to the social change around them.

So put it all together, and Orange County does not present itself as a particularly temperate climate for a liberal Protestant congregation, planted by white settlers a few decades back, decidedly out-of-step with the social and theological instincts of most remaining churchgoers in the area. Conventional thinking might lead us to conclude that a United Church of Christ congregation would be a hopeless cause in such a place.

Yet that would be a gross miscalculation. In fact the UCC planted a new congregation here in 1979.

Irvine United Congregational Church is a church passionately devoted to serving and magnifying the influence of a tiny market of persons. Pastor Paul Tellström throws out a guess that "progressive Christians" represent perhaps 1 percent of the market of would-be church people in Orange County. And yet, factor in that Irvine is the fastest growing city in Orange County and the sheer volume of people, and the possibilities add up to something. Of the two hundred thousand people who live in Irvine, thirty thousand are decent prospects for church participation. One percent of that would be three hundred. Reach a few unchurched folks, and draw from other communities—in this case as far as Huntington Beach, and this is doable.

Doable, but how did they do it?

Paul doesn't even live in Orange County. As a gay man, he doesn't really want to. He and his partner own a home fifty miles away in Pasadena, in a community with a very different personality. His partner is a realtor there. But after the long-tenure pastor of Irvine UCC resigned in order to assume leadership of the Center for Progressive Christianity, the search committee turned to Paul.

Irvine UCC's long-time pastor, Fred Plumer, had developed a strong, steady, pastor-centered liberal congregation. Attendance in worship grew to nearly two hundred under Fred's leadership, making it one of the flagship UCC congregations in southern California. The church was powerfully shaped by the strong opinions and personality of its leader. In 1992, the church declared itself Open and Affirming, one of the first faith communities in Orange County to embrace gay and lesbian people. Joan is one of the straight members today who was around in that era. She says this change functioned to encourage people to let themselves to be known without barriers, without editing. This became a blessing and an opportunity, in her view, for every person in the church, not just those who were gay. It increased the sense of freedom and authentic community available within the church, still a bit rare in the early nineties.

Irvine UCC is housed in rather odd buildings—they started with a homemade geodesic dome, built by the members themselves, from a kit. Then they purchased a temporary bank building for a dollar, cut it in half, hauled it across Los Angeles, and reassembled it on their site as a preschool and office addition. Later they added a second geodesic dome as sanctuary—a building that is worth keeping for the long haul, even as the others will need to be replaced.

Irvine UCC was a healthy congregation in many ways, with clarity of values, and lacking much history of conflict. But it was also still a pastor personality cult to some degree, left to discover if they could survive (1) without Fred, (2) in a very odd array of buildings, and (3) in Orange County.

The lay leadership recognized that for their church to grow far beyond where Fred had taken it in worship attendance, it would have to begin functioning like what is often called a program church, a larger and more complicated social system in which multiple competent leaders were present, with less dependence on the pastor to help run everything. They recognized that this would require a significant shift in leader style for their next pastor.

The basic costs of maintaining (and ultimately improving) a building suitable for an upper-middle-class suburb demanded this. In most suburbs, the long-term business models for churches of less than two hundred in attendance don't work. Additionally, the costs of employing a full-time seminary-trained pastor along with a few part-time staff would require a larger payroll for the long-term. The church feared (correctly in my opinion) that their church's failure to grow larger would leave them stuck with rising costs, which in turn could jeopardize their future and their opportunity to influence the surrounding society.

After Fred resigned, the church hired an interim pastor who loved to sing show tunes in the pulpit. In the summer of 2005, he sang *Les Miserables*, one song a week. Show tunes each Sunday in a geodesic dome. (Some of you are thinking, "Only in California.") They had good fun and held onto 130 or 140 folks a Sunday, providing a good foundation for the next era in the church's life. For an interim pastorate after a long-tenure pastor, it was a success.

In 2006, the call committee invited Paul Tellström to become their next pastor and to help them reach toward becoming something more, a church with a wider impact, a faith community built to last. So began a rather unconventional journey of a somewhat settled twenty-seven-year-old congregation with a nonresident pastor pointed toward a future that the demographics said was questionable at best. (Real life in pastoral ministry is never quite what you imagined in seminary.)

Paul secured a small apartment near the church so that he could be spared the grueling commute at least three days a week. Then half of each week, he would retreat back to Pasadena, where he could work on sermons and finish his Doctor of Ministry thesis (on the subject of preaching in order to grow a church's stewardship).

Paul framed his first challenge at Irvine as strengthening worship. The worship space was devoid of any religious symbols except for a small second-hand brass cross. The church's theological language had been largely devoid of any Christological language. Slowly Paul began to change this and to gently nudge the church toward more liturgical structure and more intentionally Christian content. He also wore a clerical robe, a first at Irvine UCC.

Paul applied great effort to artfulness in his preaching, which probably enabled him to win over some of the folks who may have been a bit unsure of the shift in the theological and liturgical tone. He continued to uplift somewhat predictable liberal social values, long treasured in the church. The members at Irvine rave about Paul's skillfulness as storyteller, with his stories tied to the biblical text for the week. One member, Joan, says, "He takes you on a journey and it sticks with you for the week. I find myself sharing (the ideas) with friends and family."

The years 2006 to 2008 were periods to add chairs, paint, update, refocus and study Alban Institute resources on growth from a pastor-centered to a program-oriented church. Music grew stronger, the services more rooted in scriptural themes. When asked to describe worship at Irvine UCC, people responded with words such as "powerful," "outstanding," "intentionality," "feeds us spiritually," and "kid-friendly." The numbers of families with small children began to rise, and with this larger and better-organized Sunday school classes.

In late 2006, Paul preached a series of sermons on progressive Christianity around the theme "Who do we say we are?" He gathered the material for the series from a survey of members about their values. At the end of the series, he said, "This is who you have said you are. This is what matters dearly to you. Now I am inviting you to step up to the plate and to share something that is precious to you." He took a quotation by David Ray from his *Big Small Church Book* and placed it front and center: "Any church that knows who it is and why it exists will figure out how to be what it wants to be." In other words, the biggest issue in a church's ministry is theological—finding a means to fund ministry is always a sub-plot. With this reasoning, Paul rallied the church around their identity as a progressive church in Orange County. The financial pledges going into 2007 oversubscribed the proposed budget by nearly $20,000.

Paul says that some folks "quietly and respectfully left" in those years, as the church began to grow, and as it shifted toward something a bit different than they had signed on for. Thankfully, the new people coming in outnumbered those going out, and the church grew steadily. The church grew steadily younger. Average worship attendance rose to 156 in 2006 and exceeded two hundred for the first time in the church's history in 2008. The 2008 attendance jump came, in part, in response to the church standing up very publicly for what they believed at a moment of significant California controversy.

As a liberal church, Irvine UCC confounded many Southern California Christians with their openness to the truth in other faith traditions. But this same openness continued to attract the people Irvine UCC wanted to attract. And then, in 2008, a little thing called Proposition 8 offered a watershed moment for the congregation.

Proposition 8 was a ballot initiative in California to define marriage as "between a man and a woman." Heavily financed by the Mormons, Proposition 8 ads began running night and day, invoking fear of what might happen to California families if gay and lesbian folks were able to legally marry. The folks in Irvine UCC found themselves unable to sit on the sidelines. Having worked through such issues nearly two decades earlier, the church was ready to rise to the call of what seemed a cut-and-dried social justice issue. In a congregational meeting, the church unanimously voted to push back and to publicly fight against the passage of Proposition 8. They marched against it. They offered their church building as an organizing point and a place to store signs and hold meetings with the Orange County anti–Proposition 8 volunteers.

Suddenly, their church was on the map. The media took notice. Other churches took notice. Other politically progressive community residents took notice. The people against gay marriage took notice. Pastor Paul began to receive hate mail, phone calls, and e-mail. Yet, in the weeks that followed, the church received new members from the Assemblies of God, the Southern Baptists, the Missouri Synod Lutherans, the Seventh Day Adventists, and the Mormons.

A couple years later, when a fundamentalist pastor in central Florida was causing global havoc with his public threat to burn a Koran, Irvine UCC decided that they would have a Koran Blessing Sunday. On this day, they blessed Korans and then sent them to several mosques in Southern California with a word of encouragement and love. This event was covered on TV and in newspapers. And, predictably, this inspired more hate mail and threats than the church's stand against Proposition 8. Two men stood guard during the service of blessing, and the police patrolled the area on heightened watch. Paul reflects, "The Islamaphobia in this country is worse than the homophobia—which I did not realize until we took this action."

Today, Irvine UCC is still growing, both in number and in the range of its ministry. It is a safe place where folks can belong even while they are talking out what exactly they believe. They insist that no matter where a person is on her or his faith journey, there is a place for them at Irvine UCC. It is a church where folks do not ever have to come to agreement. The journey, the exploration, is at the heart of the fun! Their line-in-the-sand commitments are more social justice in nature than theological.

In all of this, leadership has expanded far beyond a strong senior pastor. The church now has an associate pastor, Elizabeth Griswold, working full-time alongside Paul. In Elizabeth, the church chose to embrace a younger leader who minced no words in terms of her understanding of social justice. Elizabeth has a passion for issues far beyond LGBT equality, including the gospel implications for U.S. foreign policy. These issues challenge the Republican sensibilities of Irvine, and even of some Irvine UCC members. They are not trying to hug the middle of any road. They have embraced a role of being a voice of faith from the left in Orange County.

The moderator of the congregation is a key volunteer role in a congregational church—and the moderators at Irvine have taken that role seriously, devoting considerable time toward leading the church forward. The church was very fortunate that such leaders were available and stepped up to the plate, especially following the departure of the founding pastor. In recent years, the moderators have taken on an increasingly proactive leadership role. They do not serve as figureheads but as real conveners in a live process of give-and-take in the governance of the church and the discovery of the "what-next."

In addition, they have a fresh class of thirteen new Stephen Ministers, extending the church's ministry of one-on-one care giving beyond what two pastors can offer. There are book clubs, Bible study, youth group, pastors' potlucks, game nights, dinner groups, a knitting club, and other groups—they are working hard to cultivate multiple hubs of relationship around the personalities and passions of their community.

Nearly three hundred people now worship in three services on many Sundays, each with a distinctive style. They have a team of people making plans to tear down the one-dollar bank building and build a more permanent and architecturally pleasing administrative, classroom, and preschool space, appropriate for a growing suburban church.

But pretty suburban buildings aside, we can expect that this fellowship of eclectic and questioning folks will continue to cut its own pattern: standing up for the rights of all people and skating on the theological edge, while continuing their tradition of holding hands at the end of most services in order to sing a sentimental old 1970s chorus handed down from Bill and Gloria Gaither.

Vintage Irvine UCC.

POSTCARDS FROM IRVINE

- Accept where you are, but move forward. And do so in faith.
- Name your goals out loud. Pay attention to your goals. Then make sensible and reasonable steps to pursue them.

- Come together and then recognize why you are together! What is special about this community? What can you offer to the world?

- Know who you are and why you exist. Then be prepared to rise and fall on that knowledge.

- As you put yourself into the community, have courage to be who you are, and let your light shine!

- My job is often to lead from behind, because of strong lay leadership. (Pastor Paul Tellström)

9

THE EXCELLENT REMNANT CHURCH

Sag Harbor United Methodist, Sag Harbor, New York

> Arrived at last in old Sag Harbor; and seeing what the
> sailors did there; and then going on to Nantucket, and see-
> ing how they spent their wages in that place also, poor
> Queequeg gave it up for lost. Thought he, it's a wicked
> world in all meridians; I'll die a pagan. (Herman Melville,
> *Moby Dick*)

Sag Harbor, New York, is a seaside hamlet near the tip of Long
Island, about two hours east of Manhattan (a bit faster by Lear Jet
or helicopter). In the early 1800s it was a major East Coast port, especially for whaling ships. As the whaling industry declined, the
drunken sailors gradually disappeared, and Sag Harbor morphed
into a colony of artists and wealthy New Yorkers fleeing the intensity of the city. Today Sag Harbor is part of a string of resort villages
known as the Hamptons. The Hamptons are the playground of the
some of the wealthiest folks on earth. Steven Spielberg, Rene Zell-
weger, Jerry Seinfeld, Paris Hilton, George Soros, Billy Joel, and
Christie Brinkley all have homes out here. At a simple café in Sag
Harbor, you can run into just about anybody.

You'll probably never see any of the aforementioned at church. The very rich have one thing in common with the drunken sailors of old: a large number of them die as "pagans."

But there's more to Sag Harbor than the jet setters. In any community with folks this wealthy, there are always plenty of poor folks, with humble homes tucked away a few miles from town, working for just a little more than minimum wage, teaching in the schools, running mom and pop cafes and galleries, and managing the estates. In Sag Harbor, there is also a quiet set: young retirees and work-at-home professionals who never hit the hot parties. A growing number of folks wander out this way in order to raise families in a safe, somewhat idyllic environment, enduring a long commute back to New York three to five times a week.

The Sag Harbor Methodist Church is not quite as old as the village, but its 175-year-old white New England–style meetinghouse is a local architectural landmark. In the 1860s, 750 people belonged to this congregation. Yet, as has been the case with thousands of similar churches across the United States, the church declined over many decades, to around 150 in the 1960s, and then to the point more recently where their building finally became too expensive to maintain. Building repairs were deferred until there were only fifteen people left in a gorgeous old space that needed a minimum of $1 million in basic infrastructure work just to keep the place from going to ruin. Most of the members were into their eighth decade of life, except for one little girl in Sunday school.

The ship was going down.

Pastor Tom MacLeod came to the church in 2002. He says, "The church was dead, but no one had told them."

Tom came to Sag Harbor as a "certified lay speaker." Thousands of such persons are present all across the United Methodist Church. With shrinking churches and rising costs of ordained pastors, lay speakers are a major part of the future for the denomination as it deploys pastoral leadership to its churches. People in Sag Harbor Church assumed that Tom had been sent to close them on out. Tom went in determined to make it work. He brought an optimistic attitude and he asked the people to pray for him. They were delighted to work with him to help their church live!

Neither Tom nor Sag Harbor Church would get another shot at this. He says, "I was their last chance, and they were my only chance." This was their moment. All they had was now. Thankfully, they seized it. They had nothing to lose.

The church was known locally for two annual rummage sales and a yard sale . . . to raise a little cash. Carol, a member for twenty-five years, dreaded the rummage sales. But she usually ended up working them hard because she saw them as a way to keep her church open a little longer. During the first rummage sale after Tom arrived, he walked in and put up a poster announcing that 100 percent of the proceeds from the sale were going to missions. This was a unilateral move. In many places it would have been the beginning of the end for Tom, to announce what the church folks were going to do with their rummage sale money without first polling the church folks. But in this case, people saw that Tom was risking his own salary and that he trusted God. The rummage sale workers went with the idea. It was a hopeful moment, and a turning point for the church.

So rummage sale money at Sag Harbor, from that day forward, went for missions. Further, if the church was going to live, it would be freed from the ventilator of perpetual bazaars.

The fact that Tom was a layperson and not an ordained pastor may have played to his advantage in the early months. His assertion of leadership could not be portrayed as a clergy-lay power struggle, because it simply was not that.

Each sale day netted around $1500 for church expenses (twice a year). Tom points out that just a few weeks after the church gave up the rummage sale money, they struck a deal to house a counseling service for $1500 a month (this would be twelve times a year). A few months later, village zoning issues curtailed the rental of church space to the counseling service. (And my, are there some zoning issues in ritzy historic districts!) So they again exercised trust in God and simply gave the space to the counselors (for free). But within a few days, a playschool came right along after that looking for space. They housed them in the basement for $1500 a month. For the church, these ministry partners were like manna from heaven, confirming their faith and trust.

During Tom's first couple years, the church added "praise music" to the mix in worship, music that had a freer and more expressive tone. When they did not have live instrumentalists, they sang karaoke. And it all worked. Slowly they grew to about forty worshipers a week, the highest average attendance in at least a quarter century.

But their ancient four-hundred-seat building took entirely too much upkeep. So they decided to try to sell it and build something more practical. Tom came from a background in construction and he figured he could help them with the planning and construction of a new facility, if they could get rid of the old.

People, of course, had good memories from their old sanctuary with the morning light radiating through Victorian era stained glass. They knew that would not be able to afford to duplicate it, even on a smaller scale. So selling required some processing, some grieving. Most people at Sag Harbor, however, were able to think of the church's needs ahead of their own. So they rallied around the idea of selling and rebuilding. People credit Tom's energetic and hopeful spirit as a critical factor in anchoring the church as they moved away from a place they had called home longer than any could remember.

They knew that their church location in a prime historic district of one of the old Hamptons villages should bring a good selling price. But, on the other hand, how much market could there be for a needy church building? In early 2008, just before the real estate crash, an area resident paid Sag Harbor Methodist $2.9 million for their old building, with plans to spend several million more and convert it into a ten-thousand-square-foot palatial residence with stained glass windows and a church steeple. It would be an entertainment showplace.

As a side note: To date, this renovation has not taken place. The buyer tried to work out a deal to sell to the community library, and then to sell to a group wanting to build a large bed and breakfast. They even tried to turn it into a wallpaper factory. Nothing has worked out yet with the old building, but the United Methodists took the money and moved on!

The church spent about $600,000 for three acres of land (compared with 0.48 acres at the original site) and another $1.5 million to build a simple building that came to about sixty percent of the square footage of the original building. The new sanctuary seats 144, and comes with a fifty-car parking lot, the first in the church's history. The church was able to pay cash for all of this, and they set aside a considerable nest egg as well.

Were it not for the appearance of a buyer just weeks before the market changed, they would still be in the old building, and possibly for years yet! This story (like the ones in D.C. and Austin) is, in part, a story of the right timing with regard to real estate! They would call it God-timing.

Between the selling of the old and the opening of the new, they moved to a nearby church building, where the African Methodist Episcopal Zion congregation had recently closed. Moving from a four-hundred-seat building into a sixty-seat building immediately improved the sense of intimacy and energy in worship. It was a much simpler building, one that showed some wear and tear simply from a few years of vacancy. One very long-time member, Bruce, says that the church discovered "a greater sense of sanctuary" in this humble interim location than they had known in the previous half century at the other place. The AMEZ chapel had once been a stop on the Underground Railroad and this contributed to the sense of sanctuary.

Soon after they moved into the AMEZ building, the church adopted a Latino congregation. The United Methodist folks were still trying to find their parking spaces and which door to use, and immediately they were sharing space with another congregation. This added to the positive energy of that time.

One of the most notable elements of the Sag Harbor story is how little conflict they experienced in their rebirth—in comparison with some of the other stories in this book. I asked several folks at Sag Harbor about this lack of conflict. Tom immediately credited the excellent pastor who had come before him. In fact, his predecessor, Howard Faulkner, served Sag Harbor five years for $100 a week and gave it all back to the church. Howard at age eighty-one is still very active in the church, serving on the trustees committee and preaching twice a year. Tom knows that Sag Harbor could not have responded to his leadership in the way it did without the work that Howard had done, gently, humbly, and faithfully getting the people ready.

Another member, Frank, characterized the people who hung on at Sag Harbor as "an excellent remnant." I like that term. It applies to several stories in this book. We could devote a whole chapter to this alone, but I will keep it to a couple paragraphs here.

What are the marks of an excellent remnant?

- The people who remain have retained a vital personal spirituality, even as their church has diminished. Above all, they love God. It's that simple.

- No one person has abused his or her position and taken power over the rest in a self-serving or dysfunctional way.

- They are ready to work with a leader who is wired to challenge them to move toward God's excellent future.

- They often have the history of a pastor (before they began to grow) who worked with marked humility, faithfulness, and spiritual depth.

An excellent remnant (in church terms) is sort of like an old house that one might want to renovate, one that may look like it is falling down outwardly. But when you send in the engineer, she investigates carefully and then says to you, "This place has good bones. It will be a showplace when you are done." Excellent remnants give old churches good bones, good spiritual infrastructure for renewal.

Carol chimed in on this conversation to add that when she had come to the church in the 1980s, there were quite a few folks who would have given Tom a hard time. But by 2002, they were mostly gone. This also is a theme I have noted in other church transformation stories: churches sometimes have to lose a few certain personalities before they are ready to move forward, before they become (in Franks' words) "an excellent remnant."

Today, Sag Harbor Church is a diverse and interesting mix of people. Some have come to the area from other Long Island communities to get a little further from the city. Some have come from as far away as Antigua. They are white. They are black. They are politically all over the map. Religiously, they come from Catholic, Protestant, Jewish, Muslim, and Hindu life backgrounds. One of the most recent new members had been a Jehovah's Witness.

If you took a snapshot of everyone on the front steps after Sunday worship and then asked someone to tell you where they think these sixty or seventy smiling folks lived, the last thing you would likely hear would be the Hamptons. These are remarkably and delightfully ordinary folks. Sag Harbor has a wide range of economic levels, but any paparazzi that wanted to lurk around looking for a good photo op would probably be disappointed. Pastor Tom has been delighted by the way that strong relationships have formed between rich and poor. They minister to each other. He thinks they are a stronger church because of this. Mother Teresa would certainly agree.

Members described their church with the following statements. "Everyone fits in." "It's a land of misfit toys." "Everyone's welcome." "Leave it at the door." "Just show up." "People are real." "People accept and love each other where they are at." "Radical trust in God." "I cannot imagine anyone showing up at this church and not being welcomed and accepted."

A twenty-one-year-old woman, Temidra Willock, used these words: "Diverse, intimate, spiritually exciting." She also added that she remembers when she would have used a different set of words: "Traditional, tense, segregated." She would know perhaps better than any. You see, Kristen was the only child in Tom's first confirmation class at Sag Harbor several years ago. Young people often see reality with more clarity than the grownups. Sag Harbor Church raised her to a mature faith—even though she was the only kid they had at the time!

As of this writing, Tom has recently completed seminary. In eight years as a part-time pastor, he has helped grow Sag Harbor Church, sold the old building, designed the new, and relocated the congregation twice. He looks forward now to a new era where he will be able to better focus, and to lead them to the next level in their ministry development.

Tom says, "It feels as though my ministry is just beginning—we have a body of Christ—and there is more than me pushing here!" He feels that the biggest next challenge is developing more leaders: "It can't all come through me; we will be more powerful when God's vision is mediated through many."

Because of this tenacious, faithful church, it is a safe bet that quite a few Sag Harbor residents will not "die a pagan."

POSTCARDS FROM SAG HARBOR

- Be willing. Be willing to go along with God. Be willing to let God undo what you have done.

- Be generous and trust God.

- Talk about Jesus and his love.

- You can't out-give God.

- Prayer, prayer, prayer, prayer, patience.

10

THE CHURCH WHERE EVERYBODY GETS A HUG

St. Mark United Methodist, Sumter, South Carolina

In 1999, Telley Gadson was sent by her bishop to serve two African-American United Methodist congregations in rural South Carolina, near Sumter. Both of the churches were struggling, with a combined Sunday attendance of about fifty people. Judicatory leaders suggested that it would be helpful for the two churches to merge if they were to find a sustainable future. So, in 2002 with her guidance, both churches began to study the possibilities of merger.

Telley is a very good preacher, in much demand around her region to speak and to lead revival services. She brought new energy to both of the churches, and they began to grow under her leadership. Between 1999 and 2004, one church grew from twenty to seventy-five in attendance. The other, St. Mark, grew from thirty-five to about 130.

Rich, a member at St. Mark prior to Telley's arrival, describes those days: "We were having church, but the motivation was missing. We were going through the motions. We had thirty-five on Sunday and $70 to $100 in the plate and we thought we were doing well."

By all accounts, Telley Gadson supplied much of the motivation and the focused vision that were lacking. So far as I can tell, there was little about the vision Telley brought that differed from what most rural American churches would ascribe to, if pushed. So the vision did not really change with Telley, so much as the accountability, the energy, and the focus applied to the vision. There would be no lip service without action. In a way that perhaps only a revival preacher can do, she asked her churches to decide and to act. To act boldly in response to what they already knew! Pastor T (as they often call her) expected the best out of her people. And she usually got it.

Charismatic pastoral leadership is a factor in several of the stories in this book, but not all. In my observation, it is almost always a factor in any African American church that experiences new life. The fact that Telley was preaching and doing the same things in two places, with similar positive results, teaches us two things:

First, it teaches us that Pastor T is an extraordinary leader. What she did in her first five years in this pastoral charge was no fluke; it was replicable, because both churches grew as a result. Few pastors with two point charges will ever grow both of them at once. It is quite rare. She is the real deal.

Second, it teaches us that where there is a strong theological consensus around the church as a mission station for the lost, church transformation is easier. Telley did not come with a significantly different understanding of the faith, or a significantly different paradigm of church. Even many of the power brokers, who may have been uncomfortable with the changes and growth that they could not control, probably still agreed with most of what Telley was saying and doing, and they too celebrated the early victories.

Perhaps it was because of the growth, perhaps because of social class issues, but leaders in the smaller congregation fought the idea of merger. They were a church with quite a few college-educated professionals in a community where there weren't many such folks—and they were concerned that their church should retain their distinctive people mix. While this may sound a bit snooty when read from afar, a lot of churches would come to the same conclusion if they were honest. Telley feels that this church was the one that really needed the merger the most. But her district superintendent decided to stop pushing the idea. There seemed to be no point in forcing the matter and ending up with a bigger, divided church. So the superintendent brought the matter to a close by separating the two churches into different pastoral assignments. He then invited Telley to stay with St. Mark and work to grow it as her full-time assignment. She agreed.

Lay leadership ultimately blocked the transformation at one church and embraced it in another. Even in the black church tradition, transformation ultimately requires a team of leaders. It's not just the preacher. The pastor can kick-start it, but she cannot make the touchdown. There were places where even Jesus could do no miracles, because he experienced a hostile spiritual environment. Another way of saying this is that there is no pastor talented enough to lead transformation in some places, where the leadership can't get on board with change.

The church that resisted the merger is now about half the size it was five years ago, in large part due to poor pastoral leadership in the years since. Every time a church changes pastors it reaches into a deck of cards. They had the best. But they were not ready to follow her. Their window of opportunity opened and then it closed. Such is life.

Meanwhile, St. Mark bought twenty acres of land across the street from its historic building. The church started saving money. But these were mostly working folks, and the fund-raising was slow. By 2007, they had about $100,000 saved. And then the snakes arrived.

Snakes.

This was a rural area, and the old church building had a serious rodent infestation in the winter of 2007. Since snakes really love eating mice, they followed the mice into the church. People began running into snakes, poisonous snakes, in the church building. Finally, Telley and the district superintendent realized that the church could not continue to worship in the old building. People could not be expected to show up in a place that could not even provide a safe sanctuary in the most basic sense of the term. So the superintendent told them they needed to move to a temporary facility while they either cleared the building of its critters or made moves to begin construction on something new across the street.

When I first heard this story, it caused me to smile. Sometimes we all need something crazy in life to push us from slow motion or even inertia into action. St. Mark was moving slowly toward relocation, but they also loved their long-time home, and many of the leaders had been in no hurry about the move. The snakes were a game changer.

For most of the church members, this was no smiling matter. The whole situation was quite intimidating. They felt homeless. Having a place to call home is important to most churches, but it is perhaps even more important to the black church in America than to other groups. In the early days of the black church in America, white churches sometimes pushed African Americans around, and even drove them out of their churches, leaving them homeless, without any place to meet and without the financial resources to build a place. So the church building became a precious thing, something that might take many years to secure! The church building was one of the few things that Southern blacks might own outright. It was one of few places where black folks could gather for community events or organize for civil rights battles. More than just a house of worship!

The St. Mark members in 2007 experienced a mixture of emotions: fear (where will we go?), grief (this is the end of an era in a house of worship with really precious memories), and even embarrassment. People around town often look for something fun to talk about, even at the expense of another person's dignity. In the case of the snakes in the church, some of the members felt like they became, for a brief season, "the laughing stock of Sumter."

Their sense of spiritual focus helped them through this very difficult moment in their life together. For a couple months, they worshiped in another United Methodist church nearby. But they needed their own space. The best available space they could find was in the middle of downtown Sumter, in a former insurance office. They signed a lease, then went in and turned the largest open space into a worship center. (They do not like the term "sanctuary," as it suggests too much quiet and sleepiness. They believe worship should be vibrant and high-energy.)

As a result of this new central location (and the snake story), everyone in Sumter learned about St. Mark, if they had not already known of the church. This was a change. St. Mark had been a country chapel, in a dilapidated building, quietly out of the way, with half its people extended family. Now it was in the middle of town, not too far from the courthouse. This increased visibility caused them to attract new people and to make new relationships beyond their typical circles.

Pastor Telley took the fund-raising nationwide. She cast the vision of St. Mark all over the nation, especially appealing to churches where she had preached revivals. Money poured in from everywhere. It even came from folks in Sumter who knew of the church's challenge.

After three years meeting in downtown Sumter, in 2010 St. Mark moved into a brand new building on its twenty-acre parcel on the edge of town. This new facility sits across the street from the place where they worshiped before. The building is used seven days a week. The church gathers around two hundred for worship, but even more folks than that come through for various meetings, ministries, rehearsals, scout meetings, and so forth.

Beyond great preaching, Telley learned people's names, and worked from the earliest days at creating an environment where new things can be tried, and where each age group felt a sense of ownership in the church.

Much of the innovation energy in the early days went toward worship. Services last a little longer than two hours. Few people look at their watches. "Our best opportunity to be the church happens on Sunday morning," says Telly Gadson. "One of the things that has taken us from thirty-five to two hundred has been doing worship well. We plan some parts, but we understand that the free movement of the Spirit is the hallmark of our worship."

They added drums. The started a liturgical dance ministry, a mime ministry, new music groups with all ages. Most of this was lay-initiated, within the encouraging and expectant climate that Telley was creating. People told me, "We would always run it by the pastor; and she always said yes." Telley wanted to see a different praise team recruited from each age level.

It became a point that there were to be no age gaps in the church. And according to the laity in St. Mark, there are no gaps. In order to accomplish this, each age level was given leadership responsibility. The church started up an evening churchwide Bible study. After the teaching, they would break into covenant groups, by age level. This is reminiscent of the old southern Sunday school class system of the early twentieth century or the Methodist class meetings of the nineteenth century. These groups were organized in such a way as to keep all ages engaged, from small children to very old adults. When one class was weaker than it should be, the overseers would spend time with its leaders, or recruit new ones, to shore it up.

As they were organizing their covenant groups, one of the Bible study themes was the Lord's Prayer. They used Harold Gordon's *Focus: Living the Lord's Prayer* as a curriculum. The words used to form the acronym of that book's title (faithful, open, centered, united, and solid) became the building blocks for the covenant groups. In addition, each of the covenant groups gave itself a name, in order to foster ownership, names such as Kingdom Kids, New Generation, YAMs (Young Adult Ministry) and so forth. These covenant groups have remained a cornerstone of how St. Mark does ministry. They offer an infrastructure for the church to do everything from pastoral care to mission projects.

The members of St. Mark are adamant that their church is not a place to come and sleep. Things hop. If you walk in the door, two people will greet you, and they will help you find a place to sit. They say if you don't want to be hugged, don't come to St. Mark. One member, Richard, recalled the first time he walked into the worship service, "a feeling you can never forget, LOVE." Others agreed.

A good example of this heartfelt caring for people can be seen in the church's new HIV/AIDS Awareness Ministry. A church member who is HIV-positive shared his personal faith story with the congregation one Sunday and revealed his HIV status. This broke the ice around the issue. He invited the church to step up and love the people so easily shunned in small town South Carolina, the people folks are afraid of. In South Carolina, three out of four folks who turn up HIV-positive are black women. St. Marks wants to stop ignoring this, and to get the larger church to stop ignoring this, and to speak up.

They are starting with the creation of community classes for AIDS awareness, moving toward an HIV-positive support group next, and then, from the relationships built there, to invite people into the heart of the church's life. A good core of folks are excited about this new ministry and the opportunities to embrace folks (and at St. Mark, that means literally hugging folks) who may not experience unconditional love any other place in their life!

Twelve years into the adventure of leading St. Mark, Rev. Gadson says, "It's been a journey. But God is faithful. And we are very, very blessed."

POSTCARDS FROM ST. MARK

- Be what you want to be! Do what you want to do!
- Step out on faith! And keep looking to God!
- Believe in God and God will take care of it!
- Don't be afraid to try new things.
- Keep God first!

11

THE YOU CAN'T OUT-GIVE GOD CHURCH

First Church Somerville, United Church of Christ, Greater Boston, Massachusetts

Somerville, Massachusetts, is an old Boston inner-ring suburb, adjacent to Cambridge just a few miles from downtown Boston. It is the most densely populated place in New England, with seventy-five thousand people crammed into about four square miles. The community was settled almost four hundred years ago as a farm community. In the nineteenth century, Somerville became the industrial heart of Boston, with multiple factories and plenty of housing for workers within walking distance. By the mid-twentieth century, the factories were mostly gone and the community had deteriorated to the point that it led the nation in several alarming statistics, including per capita auto theft.

In the mid-1980s, the Boston subway came through, and a process of gentrification began, especially in the northern part of the city, near Davis Square, between Tufts and Harvard Universities. (Harvard is not in Somerville, but it lies only a mile or so beyond the city limit.) Rent control was repealed in the city, and real estate prices began to soar. By the turn of this century, new condos, coffee shops, and art studios started to pop up. The population, long mostly working class, became more mixed, as young college-educated professionals began to settle here, along with increasing numbers of university students in search of cheaper housing than Cambridge offers. Through all the change, the racial mix of Somerville has remained majority white. However, a good number of immigrants also make this home, including contingents from varied parts of Latin America and Asia.

On College Avenue, between Davis Square and Tufts, two churches have long been across-the-street neighbors: First United Methodist and First Church UCC. Both churches used to be very large in the 1930s and 1940s. Both built enormous physical plants. And decades later, both almost died. As of this writing, the Methodists have sold their building to another group and are planning to rebuild a smaller, more efficient space as they renew their life. The UCC congregation decided to stick it out in their historic space. Here is their story.

By 2004, the twentieth-century mix of people at First Church UCC was quickly passing away, and a new group trickling in, reflecting the young professionals who were steadily moving into the community. It is said that in three Sundays, you could know everybody. People report generally good memories of this time in terms of positive community spirit; but most were aware that there was only about four to five years' worth of money left, given the trends. It was assumed that after 2008 or so, the future for the church was questionable at best.

One new member from this time, Ian, shared that he and his girlfriend liked the church and chose to join despite the questions about the future. Another new member, Marc, formerly Catholic, chose this church with his girlfriend as a place where he could explore his spiritual beliefs without much pressure. They really came to enjoy the place. Marc recalls wondering, "What will we do if this church folds?" At church meetings, the attitude was "we will do this as long as we can" and "this place is something worth keeping." Perhaps because most members were relatively new and relatively transient, they were not paralyzed by anxiety. In many cases, they knew they would only be in the area a few years anyway. There was urgency and occasional sadness, but also a sense of calm. One member, Gianna, described it as a spirit of hopefulness.

In 2004, the church called Molly Baskette as their pastor on a three-fourths time basis. Molly had a two-year-old child at the time. The less than full-time contract was appealing to her. She says that she still ended up working forty to fifty hours a week, but she takes responsibility for this—the church community expected only thirty hours.

In the early days, Molly found an eclectic mix of three-dozen folks most Sundays: a blend of very old and very young people, with new faces entering regularly. It was a fun parish to serve. As the church grew younger in the first couple years, it began to capture almost a campus ministry feel, a place that created great space for asking questions and exploring ideas of faith. As the average age of attendees grew younger and younger, Molly recalls how they would show up for worship later and later. It has been common for her to look about the sanctuary ten minutes before the worship service and to see only a handful of people. They drift in late (but once there, they are often so chatty that they almost won't go home). They drift in with energy for a progressive approach to Christian faith, reflective of what one might expect from grad students at Harvard, MIT, and Tufts.

In her words, here are some of Molly's sound-bites, describing her leadership approach:

- Throw out ideas.

- We can see (open mindedness to try).

- Be flexible.

- Create urgency, but with joyfulness and lightness!
- Church belongs to the laity—we can create the future together.

So, here is some of what they tried at Somerville.

In early 2004, some of the younger members at First Somerville proposed hanging a rainbow flag on the church building. The young people then watched the old people to see their reaction. Uncertainty. The church had been officially "Welcoming and Affirming" for some time, but had never flown a flag. When, in May of that year, the Massachusetts Supreme Court declared gay marriage legal, they decided to hang the flag. At first they rotated a variety of flags, keeping something colorful and lively on the building at all times. Today, they hang only the rainbow flag, all the time.

On the first Sunday that gay marriage was legal, Molly went to city hall in a clergy robe and handed out business cards. In front of the church building, on the same Sunday, members handed out wedding favors and glasses of sparkling cider, with invitations to church. In short, the church saw the change in state wedding policy as an opportunity to jump out in front of the community to offer ministry in ways that many other churches were not ready to do. They saw gay marriage as a justice issue, as an opportunity for ministry, and as a leverage point for energizing and growing their congregation. Further, they acted quickly and decisively, when the moment came.

The new Somerville residents tend to be young, with heavy concentration in the twenty-something age bracket, a life phase that some consider the loneliest decade in American life. These folks have left family in other parts of the country (or other parts of the world); they have graduated college and left the sororities and other kinds of campus fellowship organizations in order to start a first job or to pursue a graduate degree that requires inordinate studying, often in isolation.

So First Somerville folks figured that their neighbors could use a little community, a chance to get out of their books and meet some new friends. Since the church building itself sits on a street with heavy foot traffic, four blocks from a busy subway station, they figured "Why not throw an occasional block party right in the church front yard?"

They call it "The Beautiful Day in the Neighborhood Block Party." They have thrown this party annually since 2006. They hand out flyers and door hangers up to four blocks away in each direction. Each block party will attract between a hundred and 150 people. Maybe fifty of these are from their church. The rest are neighbors. They put church brochures on a table but make the evangelism low key. The focus is more about friendship and community. They grill veggie burgers, burgers, and hot dogs. It's free: a gift to the community. (As a note, the community block party is a strategy that my church used a few years earlier when we were developing our second campus in a new neighborhood. It is a great way to meet a lot of people and begin building relationships in all sorts of communities.) In addition to the block party, they do other things each year—festivals, outreach tables, and a Stuff Swap.

A couple years back, they tore up most of the front lawn to create an organic vegetable garden. They did this again last year. This created something interesting and worthy of conversation out front—something dynamic and living, changing each week—a good contrast to the bland lifelessness of an old beige stucco church building. They give the produce away—they do not sell it. Around 10 percent of it is used for refreshments at their Sunday coffee fellowship hour and 90 percent goes to the local food bank.

What remains of the front lawn has become a community prayer garden, a place to slow down and sit down. With benches, native plants, spiritually evocative sculpture, garbage cans, and a couple outlets to charge cell phones, they seek to create a zone of hospitality and relative calm right on their busy street. They are in the process of commissioning "interactive spiritual sculpture" for this space.

In the spirit of hospitality—a major theme at First Somerville—everybody is trained as a "welcomer," with attention directed toward the front door and those who walk in. Worshipers work to corral as many folks as possible to coffee hour after the 10:00 AM Sunday service. A member named John made a point to emphasize the value of the coffee hour. "It's really worth inviting somebody to! People bring goodies, there's good coffee, people are friendly—it's a good party." Others described this time as an extension of worship, an alternative form of communion. Most will stay at least fifteen minutes. Out of ninety worshipers, it is common for two dozen to remain after an hour. One of this church's best assets, in the experience of those who belong to First Somerville, is the relationships and alliance it offers them with other fun and interesting people. Coffee hour works here because it is capitalizes on this asset and helps people tap into the relational treasures available here.

Fun is also a theme. There is a decided lack of primness at First Somerville, a slightly irreverent playfulness alongside an awareness of the Holy. Laughter punctuates the services and other gatherings. Recently, several members marched in the local Pride Parade wearing church lady hats, as an act of invitation and also a signal that this church doesn't take itself too seriously.

The Sunday morning service is now one of three weekly worship experiences the church offers. There is also a Wednesday "experimental" service at 6:15 PM, and a Thursday morning prayer service from 7:00 to 7:30 AM. During Advent and Lent, the church offers daily morning prayer time. Aware that new people often check out churches in the summer, they work especially hard at keeping sharp and creative in their worship during the summer months.

Molly describes the church's core population as "highly educated people who value spiritual community." She has worked to leverage the gifts and personalities of this community in weekly worship. Of the 140 folks active in the church, fifty are assigned one Sunday a year when they agree to write the confession and assurance, the invitation to offering, and the blessing of the offering for that week's liturgy. In each case, they are able to weave themes from the Bible readings that week, from other literature, and from their own life experience. This adds a very personal touch to worship with a special flavor that is fresh each week. People look forward to this.

And they have fun with music. As a relatively small congregation, they do not have access to big bucks to hire professional singers and instrumentalists. They hired a church member to lead and coordinate music along with a solid keyboard accompanist. And they have fun. A lot of their people have history of some kind of music lessons. People dust off French horns and offer what they can do. On any given Sunday, you might hear guitar, electric guitar, drums, bass, electric bass, cello, violin, banjo, flute, trumpet, trombone, or hand drums. There is a bluegrass band, a string band, and a soul band—not a pro among them.

Over the last few years, attendance has steadily increased, up until the time when Molly was diagnosed with cancer and she had to take a year off to get well. This was a scary moment, since their associate pastor was leaving to take another pastoral call at the same time as Molly's time away. They hired a full time "support minister" on a one-year contract to serve the church on an interim basis. The weekly average attendance went to more than one hundred for a time, before Molly's time away, with 230 on Easter 2010. Now that she is back, most expect that the church will continue to grow.

Since Molly does not want a full-time job, the church chose to hire a second pastor, an associate to work alongside her. Normally a church this size would not get two pastors, but when the senior pastor is less than full-time, different possibilities arise. Molly is determined, more than ever after the illness, to manage well her thirty hours a week, and then go home to just be Molly and Mom. As of this writing, the church is seeking to fill the associate pastor position for the next leg of their journey.

When Molly arrived, all parties agreed that the church would be broke in five years and unable to continue. Some of the members, in good humor, called this the "expiration date." Year by year, the expiration date never got closer. Somehow, at the end of each year, there was always enough to go for five more years. More recently, the expiration date has receded even further into the future, since they finished 2010 in the black—but the most critical change is not how far away that date is, but the fact that they lost track of it. They felt good momentum; and that reality began to eclipse any concern about how much money they have.

Several members acknowledge the turning point on the money situation to be something other than what you might expect. Conventional thinking would suggest that as the church grew, more money would come in, then people would relax, and that this would be the major story. In fact, the most critical shift came before they had grown, and before the additional income came in.

Molly has challenged them with the admonition that "You can't out-give God." She is fast to remind me that this is reflective of a faith that exists within the people of First Church. When they began to get close to a balanced budget, and the idea arose that they might actually be able to balance the books by diminishing missions giving, she reminded them, "God has been good to us and it behooves us to be good to others. This is what faith is, and we will be rewarded for our faith-leaping by increased revenue." So, even when the church was still bleeding their endowment each month for operational expenses, they held the line on giving to mission causes beyond themselves. In fact, even when they were still in the red, they began seeking to increase the percentage of their income that went to mission each year. They did this until the day when they were no longer in the red. And now they still seek to inch their investment in others upward each year.

Across the years, people at First Church got more comfortable with the subject of money. People began to publicly own what they give, in actual dollars, with the understanding that different folks are in different circumstances. This is not a church that teaches a rigid 10 percent tithe—even though they, like most churches, have a few 10 percenters in their midst. But neither do they treat their pledges like their private parts, to be hidden at all times. They talk about them, in actual dollars. Not to brag, but to talk about what it means to trust God. They have cultivated a culture of honestly about giving, about low anxiety, and about trust in God. Members encourage one another to give more than they thought they could. It is okay, even encouraged, for me to say, "Last year we pledged $200 a month, and it is the most satisfying check we write each month, so this year we are going to knock it up to $300. And trust. Pray for us." (To which people will giggle and perhaps applaud.) Another person can say, "Times have been tough for my kids and me, but I knew I wanted to give something. So I promised God I would give $10 a week, and we made it—we never missed the money." And so forth.

At times, when a new budget required greater congregational giving, church leaders would lay out the net difference in income required for the next year and invite people to step up and subscribe the difference. For example, if the difference was $15,000, then the focus of the stewardship campaign was around "how much do we need to increase what we are doing in order to retain this wonderful treasure?" With this kind of attitude, focusing year by year, step by step, in an atmosphere of low anxiety and good humor, they have been able to step up time and again. They now operate their ministry, and manage their building, in the black.

And so, First Church Somerville no longer has an expiration date.

POSTCARDS FROM SOMERVILLE

- Be welcoming; don't be afraid! Just welcome all!

- Live it! Don't just say it.

- When people come to your door, pay attention to them. Engage them as persons, not prospects.

- Smile.

- Align your behavior with your desire to grow.

- Trust each other. Trust those you don't know yet. Trust those who are younger. Trust the pastor. You can gain a lot by trusting people.

- Figure out what you do well, and build on that. (Music and hospitality was what we were good at.) Make yourself a better version of yourself.

12

THE COMMUNITY CENTER CHURCH
Montavilla United Methodist, Portland, Oregon

The Montavilla neighborhood of Portland lies on the outer southeast side of the city, a few blocks to either side of 82nd Avenue (Avenue of the Roses), running south from Interstate 84 a couple miles. You can live in Portland most of your life (especially downtown and to the west) and never come here. Montavilla is a sleepy, neighborly, easy-going place, with lots of green space right next to a grittier urban area. On one block it seems like you are in pristine small-town America, and on the next like you are in a struggling, earthy large city. Many of the sixteen thousand folks who live here are robust sports fans.

Historically this was a white picket fence kind of a place, a middle-class neighborhood on a streetcar line to downtown Portland. Many homes date back to the late nineteenth and early twentieth centuries. The neighborhood's last undeveloped lots filled in with houses just after World War II. Most homes are modest and many lots are quite spacious, reflecting the fact that the earliest residents came from rural backgrounds and wanted space for a garden and a couple cows. These early generations of mostly white working-class residents gave way in the late twentieth century to folks who were living a bit closer to the edge economically.

About two thirds of the area children now qualify for free or reduced cost school lunches.

In more recent times, the area gained notoriety as Portland's red light district, complete with drugs, prostitution, and gangs. The Interstate 5 corridor is notorious for the sex trafficking of underage girls up and down the West Coast, and many of these girls ended up on 82nd Avenue for a time, in the heart of Montavilla. When 82nd Avenue was designated a prostitution-free zone by the city, many of the sex workers ended up on side streets, to the consternation of the young families in the cottages behind the white picket fences. The image of the middle-class sixth grader waiting for a school bus, fifty feet from the older teenager waiting for her next job, fifty feet from the homeless woman sleeping in an alleyway— this is Montavilla's convergence of people in the starkest of terms.

By the year 2000, a wave of new middle-class residents were steadily purchasing and renovating old homes in several areas, driven by the affordable prices compared to other parts of Portland and the central location, with good proximity to downtown, the airport, and all of the east side. At the same time, increasing numbers of immigrants begin moving into area apartments. A few trendy businesses entered into the mix alongside the pawnshop variety. Storefront Muslim prayer centers began to pop up, complementing the traditional churches.

My own experience of the neighborhood—great coffee and bubble tea to be found, a mixture of ages and races, highly visible young adults, many with highly visible tattoos. I took a walk here with a friend on a rare warm and sunny February afternoon and found something interesting around every bend. In fact, I saw what appeared at first to be the largest house cat I have ever seen, napping in the sun. Then we realized that it was actually a raccoon napping right on somebody's front lawn. A reminder to us that this city is surrounded by some of the best natural terrain on the planet!

Montavilla United Methodist Church is about as old as the neighborhood. The church was established in the early 1890s, just after the completion of the Transcontinental Railroad ignited a population boom in Portland. While Oregonians were never as religious as the folks back east, the churches came with the original settlers. Methodists were at the forefront of the Christian evangelization in Oregon in the nineteenth century. Throughout the twentieth century, however, they and most old-line Christian groups diminished as a percentage of the population. Today, less than one in four Oregonians have any formal affiliation with a religious group. Even fewer actively participate in a congregation. In such a nonreligious environment, the ministry of even a long-established church can easily become invisible to the community, and the community largely invisible to the church.

As Montavilla United Methodist Church entered its second century of life, the church had settled into a long, slow decline, with median age creeping upward and the total number of active participants creeping downward. Nonetheless, many members and church families have remained a part of the church across multiple generations. This contributes to what one young man who grew up here would summarize as a "church that is tightly connected."

Montavilla experienced a series of difficult pastoral tenures in the last twenty or so years. This is common in declining congregations located in downscale parts of town.

Such churches may get very little "new blood" into leadership and can become places where new ideas are too easily shot down and where all clergy are measured against Reverend So-and-so, who served the church back in the day. When such churches get labeled as *low potential*, this in turn may affect the care that goes into matching pastors with the church's real needs. If such a church keeps a decent pastoral salary, it can become an easy place for the bishop to park tenured pastors coasting toward retirement or those who need a quick place to land after they run into conflict in other places.

Put all that together and you have a recipe in such churches for a series of relatively short, ineffective, and often conflicted pastoral relationships. Such a church may take a black eye and get labeled as a problem child, when in fact the dysfunction is larger than simply the congregation.

This happened in Montavilla. Their bishop recognized it and sought to stop the cycle. He tried to send them a pastor who could help them move forward out of their funk, a pastor freshly trained in leadership skills for congregational revitalization.

But what was supposed to be the turnaround moment for Montavilla went awry. The church endured yet another difficult pastorate, this time complicated by some of the new pastor's personal business and the entangling of a few church members. It became a mess—perhaps the worst mess yet! A mediator was called in. There was a good chance that the church would have continued to weaken to the point that it would be unlikely to do much more than coast into its eventual grave.

With the leadership embroiled in conflict, some of the best and brightest members were leaving, either to catch their breath or to manage their sanity. Others who hung around dreaded church meetings and often skipped them. Sunday attendance dropped into the seventies, a very tiny presence given the size and the maintenance cost of their buildings. The number of giving units dropped by half to about seventy. The church had to spend endowment principle simply to repair the leaky roof.

Enter Laura Truby. Laura was sent to Montavilla in 2007 not as a messiah pastor fresh out of special training to grow the church, but as a healing pastor, skilled as an intentional interim pastor going into a devastated congregation.

Laura spent two years with the church. When she arrived, the wounds were fresh, and people were mad at one another. During this time, she listened and affirmed the gifts of people. She treated the church not like problem children but like a group of people with high potential. She respected them and accorded them with dignity. She told them they were good people, people who mattered to God. She told them that what they do matters to God, to one another, and to the neighborhood. It was truth that these folks desperately needed to hear.

Telling this reminds me of a pastor friend who would say to his church, every time he saw someone doing something good or right,

"That's the kind of place this is," until one day that was indeed the kind of place it was.

We are talking about a congregation's rediscovery of self-respect and high expectations of itself.

Laura oversaw a process of mission and vision discernment, taking seriously the input of each person. From this work, the following key elements of church mission-identity took root: (1) growing closer to God and one another and (2) making a difference in the neighborhood. (It may sound simple, but, folks, this doesn't have to be complex!)

From there, they took a series of baby steps, each of which increased the church's courage to take a next step.

The first step that folks recall about their journey back to congregational health relates to their choosing to volunteer at a small homeless shelter for families. The shelter holds up to five families at any given time. The church, along with many other community groups, volunteered to take one weekend every two months—a manageable commitment—in which they (1) prepare meals for the shelter guests, (2) provide transportation from the night shelter to the day shelter (different facilities, apparently), and (3) designate one person to spend the night as a shelter host for Friday and Saturday evenings. They also offer transportation to from the shelter to Montavilla Church on Sunday for any shelter guests who would like to come.

This simple, steady, and tangible commitment to compassion with neighbors beyond the church walls provided a good move toward answering the call to make a difference in their neighborhood. Apparently it also made as much of a difference inside the church community as beyond.

Next, the church began to share its building with the community—a very pleasant space. First, the neighborhood association needed a meeting place with more parking. The church supplies one of its members as a host/greeter for each monthly gathering. This small act of neighborly hospitality began to give the church a much greater visibility in the community.

In the summer of 2008, the church started an annual Free Day for the neighborhood. They give away clothes, plants, and household items along with a hot breakfast. In 2011, they added additional services on the Free Day, including haircuts, pedicures, resume writing and copying, street yoga, knitting lessons (with yarn and needles to take home), and a simple cooking class. A member of the church community staffs each service station. In the late fall, the church hosts a Winter Free Day focused on coats, sweaters, and blankets, given along with free hot chocolate, coffee, and snacks.

When a nearby church's building burned, the leaders of that church (La Rocha) came to Montavilla UMC because of its reputation as a place that hosted others. Iglesia La Rocha started worshiping in the Montavilla UMC facility in 2010.

Meanwhile, another congregation, the Church of Tonga, has worshiped in the church facility for more than a decade. When the Tongan church nearly lost their parsonage to foreclosure, the Montavilla UMC folks began fund-raising to help pay off the mortgage.

Meanwhile, as the church moved beyond its time of conflict, the sense of joy in the worship and fellowship gatherings just soared. A real sense of healing came. In the Christian tradition, we would look beyond simply the gifts of an effective interim pastor to fully explain this—we would also point to the mystery of the Holy Spirit. Finally God just got into the house in a fresh way, enabling the church to let go of recent pain and bitter experiences, freeing the church to embrace the joy of loving and serving in relatively simple ways.

With each new success, the momentum began to turn like a flywheel, leading to the next good thing. In many cases, these were member-initiated endeavors. In an environment of increased self-esteem, people began to take risks and try things, with the trust that the pastor and the church leaders would celebrate and encourage such initiative and not seek to control or limit it.

As a result, the church became a full-fledged community center for Montavilla, hosting or sponsoring the following things:

- Various support groups
- The Council for Prostitution Alternatives
- The neighborhood association
- Food ministries (both a coop and food bank with monthly hot meal)
- A community liturgical dance group
- A community choir
- A community orchestra
- The Filipino cultural association
- Art shows
- A creative writing group
- A couple book clubs
- An annual poetry event

They are also seeking to begin hosting an AlAnon group.

It should be no surprise that worship attendance has been on the upswing for three years now. Offerings increased to the point that the church ran a surplus in 2010, in the midst of the recession, an amazing turnaround from three years prior, even as the church began to support so many new causes and ministries. These institutional kinds of health indicators are up because the church has been focusing first on being church, both within the walls and beyond. Montavilla Church illustrates beautifully what I have said for years in my paraphrase of Matthew 6:33: "Seek first the reign of God, and attendance and money will take care of themselves."

A praise band started, sharing drums with La Rocha. The creative writing group began to publish Advent and Lenten devotional booklets and a quarterly arts publication. A group called WOW (With or Without) started for young couples (twenties and thirties mostly) either with kids or without. This was the idea of one church member—and in an environment of increased self-esteem, they just went for it, and a new ministry took root! More than two dozen people often gather for WOW-sponsored events. Because of the new people who came into the circle from WOW, the church held a confirmation class in 2009 from which eighteen young people were confirmed. In the wake of this, an active youth ministry emerged.

As all of this was unfolding, in mid-2009, Laura passed the baton to Peg Lofsvold, Montavilla's current pastor. Intentional interim pastors often need two years to take a troubled church to a stable and healthy place. Often the first year is about debriefing and building trust with the interim pastor so that positive steps and decisions can occur in year two. Peg Lofsvold came to a very different congregation than had existed two years earlier. She stepped into a context of positive energy and momentum.

The child-care program that has rented space for years will be leaving soon, and the church is dreaming about ways to repurpose the space for community ministry. Ideas range from laundry and showers for the outdoor neighbors to an indoor play park for area children.

At the same time, we should be candid here to say that Montavilla is still a church in the process of transformation. In fact, one of the reasons I chose their story is because they are still relatively young in the newest era of their church's story. Pentecost is just really starting to unfold here. It's an interesting season, and a bit scary for some.

There are often homeless people in and around the church building before and after evening meetings. Sometimes they are new faces. Sometimes they are rough looking. Therefore, the church is intentional about greeting folks who are arriving at the church outdoors, in the parking lot, and walking them into the building, past any scary-looking characters.

In early 2011, a homeless couple (a man and a woman) started camping in the churchyard. Understandably a few church members were unhappy about this development for a number of reasons, ranging from safety to aesthetics to the condition of the grass. Peg decided to welcome them to church rather than run them off the yard. They, in turn, began to talk with their tribe about their church and the caring they experience there. By late spring, about a dozen homeless folks were in worship each week. The church held a community barbeque on the front lawn and a couple dozen homeless folks came. Now when it rains (and this is the Pacific Northwest, folks), it is common to see homeless neighbors on the church's covered porch, because they feel safe and welcomed here.

On Pentecost Sunday in summer 2011, six persons joined the church: two retirees from back east, a single Asian immigrant woman, a single young Anglo man in his twenties, and the homeless couple mentioned above. Then a few weeks later, two dozen more folks joined—the entire La Rocha congregation—adults, teens, and older children—along with their pastor (now a candidate for ordained ministry in the United Methodist Church).

The church is taking on the ethnic flavor of Montavilla neighborhood. There will be occasional tensions with this level of people diversity. But the people of Montavilla Church simply have to work out any tensions that this diversity presents. And as they do so, they model for their whole neighborhood how diverse persons build positive community together.

Pastor Peg heard one church member after another talking about reaching the community. Well, by God's grace, they began to really do so! But she cautions, "Be careful what you wish for!" This church made a wish, and God literally gave them Pentecost.

Pentecost is chaotic, a little messy. Not everyone is pleased with the new Montavilla Church. There is murmuring, even as I write this page.

The murmuring will pass. It may blow up into a full-fledged fit of drama, or it may just die away in a few months. But they will move past it. The church is now probably too healthy for this to devolve into what happened at Calvary Baptist in D.C. But mutinies are normal in church transformation, and some pushback should be expected by people who have been around a long time and are not counting on this many new people coming onto what has been their turf.

What has happened here in the last few years is nothing short of a miracle. It all happened without flash, without a big budget, with ordinary people in an extraordinarily ordinary neighborhood. It happened with love, listening, praying, with respect. The church chose community, both within and without. They chose frontier. They chose fun. Their growth has been organic and a natural response to an increasingly healthy church culture.

Pastor Peg sums up her job as follows: "to name what God is doing, to connect people to it, and to keep the vision in front of them." She is holding them accountable to the vision—but she loves the fact that she doesn't have to push, that the initiative for one new idea after another comes from grassroots members and others. There are thousands of churches in similar situations to Montavilla across the United States. If healing and new life can happen here, it can happen in any of those places!

POSTCARDS FROM MONTAVILLA

- Have a free day! Forget the rummage sale where you haggle for money in the parking lot! Give the stuff away!
- Be transparent. Be sure that people know what's up! Good communication lowers anxiety.
- Be open to change—look for ways to accept change!
- Don't give up! Don't abandon ship!
- Look to your brothers and sisters in other churches to help you with community ministries.
- It's kinda scary.
- But let's do it anyway.

13

THE PENTECOST CHURCH

Clinton Avenue United Methodist, Kingston, New York

In the Dutch Colony that would eventually become New York State, the three original major settlements on the Hudson were New York City, Kingston, and Albany—each originally known by other names. For a short time, during the Revolutionary War, Kingston (located in between the other two) was the capitol of New York, but then the British burned it down (as the British were so prone to do in those days.)

Today, the oldest section of the city of Kingston—where the Dutch originally settled—is called Uptown. Many of the buildings that were built back after the British invasion in the late 1770s remain and lend an old-city feel to the place. This neighborhood is listed in the National Register of Historic Places as the Stockade District. As the neighborhood slipped into disrepair in the 1970s, various attempts at new development became flashpoints for battles on architectural preservation. While Uptown has its charm on a few key streets, the larger area continues to struggle economically, especially outside the immediate historic district. In recent years, with the local demise of IBM, many families have fled the area looking for work in other places. This has, in turn, further destabilized the local economy and depressed real estate prices.

Most churches in this part of the world are shrinking and seeking, at best, to hold on. In an environment where there is a diminishing pool of churchgoers for old-world Protestant churches, those with good looks (architecture) and money (endowment) often more easily manage to survive as many of their peer congregations fade away. There are several old churches in Kingston, a few of which continue to thrive (or at least pay bills) as regional, albeit historic, congregations.

There are two United Methodist congregations, four blocks apart. One is in the heart of a small, but sexy, historic district (Uptown). The other is slightly outside of it. In the minds of many residents, the neighborhood is synonymous with crime and mischief. This is the story of the latter church, the one with the less prestigious address—Clinton Avenue United Methodist Church.

Clinton Avenue had been steadily losing ground for as long as anyone can remember. Nonetheless locals can still recall people worshiping in the balcony as recently as the 1980s. But after the IBM plant closed in the 1990s and the church's neighborhood surroundings deteriorated, Clinton Avenue found itself having trouble competing with the other churches for worshipers. They shifted to a part-time pastor, began to get behind on building maintenance, and soon began to run out of people. The Episcopal and Old Dutch churches and the other Methodist church each continue to serve a dwindling base of bluebloods, white-collar folks, and descendents from local Protestant families. Clinton Avenue, on the other hand, lost its base.

The final closing of the local IBM factory in 1994 provided the tipping point that sped up the decline. One-fourth of Kingston's population disappeared that year. By all reasonable expectations, Clinton Avenue Church should have been gone by the turn of the century.

But the last few folks, the hangers-on, hung tough.

In 2004, the bishop sent Darlene Kelley to be the last pastor of Clinton Avenue Church. Nine elderly worshipers showed up on July 3, 2004, to welcome her. They gathered in the basement, since the utilities to operate there cost less and the sanctuary needed ceiling repairs. Their attitude was that they had enough money for eight of the nine of them to be buried before the last one standing turned out the lights. It was hard to imagine that Clinton Avenue Church would ever need the sanctuary again, and so it was also hard to mobilize the money and will to repair it. These nine people were the caretakers of a huge crumbling complex, complete with a gymnasium and a decrepit pipe organ.

However, the church housed a daily soup kitchen ministry started in the late 1980s as the brainchild of a local restaurant owner. The soup kitchen fed between fifty and one hundred people daily. The soup kitchen was largely disconnected from the worshiping congregation, but Darlene decided it was a place where she should hang out—especially if she was to pastor this community. After all, she had come from the restaurant business prior to getting into the church business. And so Darlene went to the soup kitchen every day because it seemed to be where the life was.

This simple choice by Darlene Kelley changed everything.

She began to make friends and, in every case, to invite them to church. Darlene has perfected the art of constantly inviting people to church without scaring them away. She does this in an endearing way that, to many folks, communicates that she cares. When I visited with Darlene in the summer of 2011, she estimated that for seven years, she had invited at least one person a day to Clinton Avenue Church—probably more than two thousand people. And several hundred of these said "yes," and dared to walk in to worship.

But I am getting ahead of myself.

When the first folks from the soup kitchen began to show up for worship with the Clinton Avenue congregation in 2004, some of the "final nine" were not ready to receive the neighbors. Attendance bounced up a little in the early days of Darlene's ministry. . By fall 2004, they had upped the number of church bulletins to twenty-five a Sunday. But there was always tension, especially with a couple of the church members. One woman, Deb, a soup kitchen regular, remembers Darlene's invitation to her like this: "I need you to come to church to help me." Darlene said that seeing Deb in church each week provided a comfort to her for all that she faced in trying to turn this church toward community.

Late that first summer, Darlene worked out a deal with the county officials to have inmates from the county jail paint the church gymnasium. The trustees released some of the dwindling endowment funds to have the sanctuary painted and cleaned. By October they were able to move back upstairs and worship in the sanctuary. The organ got repaired and they began looking for an organist.

Then one afternoon, Darlene was returning to Kingston from an out-of-town meeting, in an exceptionally good mood. She says she was singing hymns all the way home. But when she pulled up in front of the church building, she saw chains on the sanctuary doors. It was not entirely clear what the reason was for the chains—a safety issue or a hospitality issue—but the message was pretty clear to the soup kitchen folks and anyone else who happened to pass by—"This church is closed for business! Keep out and stay away!"

Darlene was deeply troubled by this and felt herself driven to go and pray, immediately. To just go right then and pray! She entered the building by another door and did a very odd thing—she climbed as high as she could go in the building, as if to step above the fray so to have a long talk with God. She rushed up the stairs, gasping for breath, and entered into the space behind the organ pipes. And there she began to pray. Darlene is a woman of prayer, but this was a prayer unlike most prayers. Head in her hands, she prayed with agony, for God to show her what to do, to show her a way forward, how to lead this church to welcome its neighbors.

And then she saw a vision.

In her mind's eye she saw the key to the lock on the chains: she saw it in the top drawer of the church secretary's desk. Immediately she climbed down out of the organ pipes and went to the church office. Upon opening the drawer in the desk, there was the key, exactly as she had seen it in her prayer vision. Taking the key, she walked around to the front doors and, sure enough, the key opened the lock!

Just as she was taking the chains off, hoisting them around her shoulders like a chain link stole, she looked up to see a few members of the church walking up the street toward the church—including the man who had put the chains on the doors! They were arriving for a church meeting, the meeting to talk about hiring an organist. That meeting was about to go off the script as a turning point moment for this church! After a brief confrontation on the sidewalk in front of the church with the man and "a small battalion," Darlene headed back up into the organ pipes to pray some more as people arrived for the meeting

Folks, you can't make this stuff up.

When Darlene came back down for the meeting, two simple words kept echoing in her soul: "Love them. Love them. Love them. Love them." She says this focus on love cast out her fear and gave her the courage to face the group and say what she had to say.

There are varying memories of what got said in that meeting. "Somebody that looked like a drug addict sat next to me in church Sunday." "Check the marquis outside. It does not say Clinton Avenue Country Club!" "We have to love folks and open wide our doors."

People were a bit stunned that Darlene was so direct. At one point she moved around the room from person to person hugging them one after another, saying to each, "It's all about love and it starts with us." Of the twenty or so folks who came to this church meeting, all are still around except for four who walked out that night and haven't yet been back. It was apparently an awkward meeting, but a pivotal one. While few folks talk about it, no one present will ever forget it.

And a new church emerged from it, a Pentecost church. Not a Pentecostal church—although visions of keys in drawers does certainly have a certain Pentecostal flavor. Clinton Avenue is not Pentecostal, but they became a Pentecost place: a place where the Spirit of God began to break down barriers between people and create a fellowship of the least likely folks that one could imagine allying together in community. The members of this faith community re-port that they cannot imagine any person walking into their midst and not receiving a warm welcome. As the barriers came down, people began to experience God's grace in their lives and to be transformed by it.

Today, five years later, Clinton Avenue is a motley cohort of sev-enty or so persons most Sundays. Hundreds of new folks have come through the church's doors, but most are transient, living at the lowest rungs of the economic ladder in Kingston. They lose jobs often. They have to keep moving. They flee drug dealers and abu-sive boyfriends. They go to jail or back home to parents in another place. Thus, the majority of the folks this church has reached are no longer around. But they have each been blessed, and they carried that blessing with them to other places!

With this kind of people turnover, the church finds itself per-petually short on cash. And yet they make a habit of trusting God to provide for their needs as a church rather than spending valuable energy and church-life time worrying about money.

They are responsible for a lot more church building than they need. But they tell me the building is solid and, for now, is not draining cash too badly. Darlene, seeking to discover ways that they could be better stewards of the large facility, made an appointment with the county commissioner for social services. She asked him and others, "What would you do with this building if you were me?" Of the suggestions received, the one that stuck was the idea to create and house a "second-chance home for pregnant teens." As of this writing, the church was working to create a space to house six pregnant girls. All of the funding for this is coming ex-ternally. In addition, in the renovation they are addressing some wiring issues that the church otherwise would have had to repair on its own.

The soup kitchen is still going strong, serving about twelve hundred meals a month, Mondays through Fridays at noon—fewer at the start of the month after people's checks go out, but increasing during the course of the month to more than eighty a day by month's end. Some who come are homeless, others living off the street, barely living. About half the folks have drug and alcohol issues.

A Narcotics Anonymous group was introduced in late 2004. It meets on Friday and Sunday evenings. There was some alarm at first about an NA group at the church. Someone mentioned, "We had an AA group back in 1965 and someone broke a lamp." They worked through the idea and chose to welcome this new ministry into the facility. The NA group now often uses the gym and stage for big community parties. In addition to NA, a couple dozen people now stay after lunch on Tuesdays, Wednesdays, and Thursdays to study for their GED (a program added in 2005). On Fridays after lunch, there is a legal clinic. A Cub Scout troop is forming. From such community groups and gatherings, everyone gets an invitation to church; and quite a few have come in and joined.

Darlene says, "For a while I had two congregations in one. But then, in time, the Harley guy helps the little old lady back to her pew after communion. To know you is to love you. If I look into your eyes I am not going to be afraid of you any more. It just takes a while."

In the meantime, she advises, in the transition season, when you are caught with two tribes of people trying to figure out what to do with one another, what to say to each other, how to be church together, the best thing to do is just hug everyone who comes in the door, and to model the community you seek to create.

One day there was a street fair on Liberty Street, and Darlene saw an inactive church member, who had been active some years before as a person of a different gender. Her name was now Candy. Candy was homeless at the time. Darlene walked up and said, "You must be Candy. I am Pastor Darlene Kelley." Another pastor in town had referred Candy to go see Darlene; so Candy responded, "I have been meaning to come talk to you." Darlene made her usual ask: "I'd like to invite you to come to church tomorrow morning at 11 AM." (Thankfully, Darlene has not read the book that says postmodern people don't want to come to worship. When Darlene writes her book it will be to say, "They are just dying for an authentic invitation.") Candy expressed her appreciation for the invitation but said, "I am not so sure, because I am different." Darlene's quick response was "So? You let me worry about that. You get up and get dressed in whatever you want to wear, and come to church."

Candy waited one week, but then, with God's help, she took Darlene up on her invitation. When she walked in, the only thing anyone seemed to care about was that she was there. Everyone seemed so happy to see her. It was a watershed moment for Candy, and also for Clinton Avenue. In 2007–08, Darlene and Candy put their heads together and decided to lead Clinton Avenue to become a Reconciling Church, a United Methodist church that explicitly welcomes gay, lesbian, bisexual, and transgendered people into full participation in church life.

As Candy was telling me this, Darlene interrupted to underline this fact: "The Gospel message is the cornerstone of all of this. One sacrifice for all of us! For ALL of us! We pray for our church and surrender it to God on a daily basis."

As I chatted with several Clinton Avenue members, one young man, Eliot, was a bit quiet. The group asked him if he had anything to share with me. He said he had come the first time for a church dinner. He was homeless at the time and relatively new to town. His mother had abandoned him and his father. The church drew him in, and he came back and then joined the church about a year ago. The sense of belonging he has discovered has been amazing for him. The best surprise came last Christmas when, for the first time in a long time, he felt he had a family again—and Clinton Avenue was it!

Christmas Eve services bring the largest crowds of the year, always more than a hundred people. And every year, for quite a few folks, this *is* their family Christmas gathering.

But don't think all of the happy stories are reserved for the newcomers who have been blessed here. The handful of old timers who stuck around through the church transformation can also report personal transformation. Eunice was one of the nine present on Darlene's first Sunday. Eunice summed up her story like this: "I have lived a good life, but for too long I lived with pride. And the pride had to go." She recounted a moment a few years back when she was unable to open her mouth to invite a man to church. She was too proud to admit she even went to church. And then she shared how, one day, she experienced "the baptism of the Holy Spirit," and how, that day, her tongue was *untied*. She spoke in unknown tongues at the time, but she also found herself able finally to speak freely to people in English and welcome them to church, all kinds of people.

Now Eunice stations herself at the front door of the church on Sundays so that she can greet everyone who walks in. She shared how just the preceding Sunday a man had walked up the steps tentatively. She greeted him, and he explained that he had just come up from under the bridge. He was homeless. Eunice brightened up, looked him in the eye, and said, "You are welcome here." And with that, his shoulders lifted, he took his bulletin and walked in the door like he belonged to this church.

That is how Clinton Avenue added its latest new community member. It is a good bet that there will be hundreds more coming along behind him.

POSTCARDS FROM CLINTON AVENUE UNITED METHODIST

- God loves us all! God needs us, too!
- Get a pastor who's an optimist and who accepts everybody!
- I have been more social than I've ever been since I came to this church.
- Come to church! Have I invited you to church yet? We want you! We need good people like you!

14

THE CHURCH WITHOUT WALLS
Worship @ the Water, Pensacola Beach, Florida

About ten years ago, my first book, *Fling Open the Doors,* shared the story of how Gulf Breeze United Methodist Church in north-west Florida planted their second campus. I served as the planter and pastor to the faith community that formed at that campus, known then as the Community Life Center and, later, simply as the Soundside Campus. Soundside has been a steady and solid ministry, with weekly worship attendance at around a thousand a week for the last several years. Gulf Breeze Church spent a small fortune planting Soundside. The whole project started as a facilities expansion for our church in a second site after we had been unable to acquire adjacent land at the original campus. Soundside is exactly eight miles from the original church campus. Cost for the land and first phase of building amounted to $3 million in late 1990s dollars. The $3 million only got the doors open. It did not include the start-up money that gave me a staff of six to run a multifaceted seven-day-a-week program at the Community Life Center. It did not cover two parking lot expansions in two years or the addition of the second floor or all the upkeep and facility upgrades of the dozen years since opening. There is nothing abnormal about any of this expense—it's how we do church most of the time in the United States.

In contrast to churches in the developing world, in America we have mastered the art of expensive church. So often when a church no longer can afford the pricey, high-maintenance building or the full-time union-card-carrying clergyperson as pastor, they conclude that they need to close. No church in Cambodia would ever draw this conclusion. But I digress.

You might be interested to know that Soundside Campus has a little known baby sister, born three years later on a shoestring budget, a faith community that has come to offer a persuasive alternative to big budget church.

I helped to plant this new community in 2002 just as I was leaving Gulf Breeze to go to work for my bishop. One evening in the winter of 2002, I met with a group of maybe twenty folks, at their request, in one of the beach restaurants to dream about a third campus of Gulf Breeze Church, a church without walls. Pensacola Beach is a small city on a barrier island across a bridge from Gulf Breeze. Pensacola Beach had two churches up until then: a small United Church of Christ congregation and a Roman Catholic parish. At least 90 percent of residents were active in no church whatsoever. Beach people are different than mainlanders in enough ways that we knew that it would take a specialized ministry initiative to serve them well. The dreamers who gathered at the restaurant were ready to work together to create a new and distinctive faith community. They wanted to call it Worship at the Water. That was later shortened to W@W.

Our first W@W service on Pensacola Beach was my last Sunday on the pastoral staff of Gulf Breeze. We gathered at 8:00 in the morning to avoid both the hot sun and the Sunday beach traffic that would soon create gridlock. I preached to 150 people who showed up in the outdoor beach bar at Flounders Restaurant on Pensacola Beach. Several stayed for brunch afterwards, confirming for the restaurant management that this deal with the Methodists was indeed a win-win.

One Sunday during that first summer, a drunk man, who had fallen asleep in the wee hours of the morning, woke up on the beach beside the restaurant and found himself in church. Someone handed him a cup of coffee. (The hospitality at W@W was good from day one!)

People worshiped around aluminum pub tables with a gorgeous view of the Santa Rosa Sound. The band was assembled from among talented folks in and about Gulf Breeze Church who were not currently in the church's other worship bands. All the fledgling worship community asked of the clergy was that we send someone to preach each week. When it rained, the restaurant had a covered area where folks could squeeze in and glass garage doors that could go down to insulate from the cold when necessary.

I led services a few times that summer, but since I was no longer officially on staff, I quickly handed it off to Tom Sharron, one of the associate pastors. Tom was the first real pastor to the community.

If Soundside is the yin, W@W is the yang. These two faith communities are part of the same overall church, the same multisite network, with the same mission and values—and yet their style and strategy are vastly different.

- Soundside started as part of an all-church initiative, complete with a big capital fund campaign. W@W started quickly and simply as an idea that bubbled up among some of the Pensacola Beach members in our church.

- Soundside cost $3 million to start. W@W cost nothing but a few bucks for coffee and donuts on day one—everything else was borrowed or donated, including the time of the people involved.

- Soundside had a seven-day-a-week campus with a variety of community ministries. W@W had a trailer (eventually) and met outdoors in the beach bar of a local restaurant.

- Soundside had an elaborate children's church. At W@W, kids and grown-ups are all together in the worship time, except during the sermon, when the kids gather over by the restaurant's volleyball court for their story time.

- Soundside was a church designed for a suburban mentality, for mainlanders. W@W was designed for the beach people, the folks on Santa Rosa Island, many of whom would never wander into any church or, even less likely, travel across a bridge back to a conventional church.

But we made at least two mistakes when we started W@W: (1) We failed to assign a pastor to at least twenty hours a week to build the ministry, corral people, and develop a church on the beach. (2) We envisioned it as a seasonal thing with a winter sabbatical—which ended up killing momentum and continuity year after year.

Since the project was conceived in such a minimalist way, we saw it mainly as an auxiliary worship service. In its first few years, attendance would rise occasionally to two hundred in the summer, and then they would take the winter sabbatical, only to have to start over again the next year. By 2008, the whole thing was tired, underdeveloped, and endangered. Attendance had been hanging between forty and fifty people for a couple years. The executive pastor at Gulf Breeze who had been leading the services moved to another church, and someone needed to take the reins. Herb Sadler, the Gulf Breeze senior pastor, approached associate pastor Jack Kale and asked him to go to the beach to pinch hit for a few months. Jack agreed, but on the following conditions:

- It would be a trial assignment, only for the summer of 2009.
- He would be released from all other pastoral responsibilities so that he could give his full attention to building a faith community on the beach. "If I am going to do it, that's all I am going to do."
- At the end of the summer, they could decide the future of W@W, knowing that they had given it a real chance.

A little should be said about Jack Kale. He came to Gulf Breeze in 2008. He previously led an extraordinary revitalization of a small-town church in southern Alabama. But in the course of that very competent work, Jack began to question the whole worship-driven, business paradigm of North American church. At the time, he had read nothing yet on the concept of missional church. He just felt something was wrong. Like the wagon was pulling a horse!

Jack looked at W@W and his first instinct was that "these people need a pastor." He knew that W@W had to be more than just a worship event, but a true faith community in every sense, with opportunities for serving others and for committing to something less erratic and haphazard.

At the start of his first summer (2009), Jack started calling folks to get a band together. He did not find an energetic response, but rather, a sense of duty and hassle. So he gathered some of the musicians from previous seasons and said, "It sounds like some people are doing this out of duty. If that is the case for you, please walk away with my blessing. But if you are in, I want you to know that I am going to be the pastor at W@W and not run off quickly after the service to another campus." With that commitment, several of the musicians found new energy and vision for the whole enterprise.

Jack began showing up on the beach at 6 AM with the first volunteers each Sunday—he feels that this kind of presence is necessary in order to keep volunteers energized, since he is the only paid staff person. He asks, "Why should the volunteers show up at that hour, and the paid guy come in two hours later after all the set-up work is done?"

The new energy caught fire with others, and attendance quickly jumped past two hundred that summer, with crowds as large as W@W had ever seen: all ages from the very young to the very old. When August came, things were going well, so they decided to give it another two months. In each service, Pastor Jack gives out his text number and asks people to put it into their phones and text him their names, telling him that they were present. This is how he does visitor registration so that he gets their contact info directly into his cell phone. He then says, "Whenever you have a need for a pastor, please text me. I want to be your pastor." He reports that there has been virtually no abusing of this access to him and that it has helped to build a sense of authentic community and caring very rapidly.

I asked him, "Jack, how many numbers are in your cell phone?" He had not thought about it. Based on three to four new numbers a week for a hundred weeks, I asked if he had 350–400 phone numbers. He first said "No way." Then he thought about it and said, "Maybe that many."

Not bad for two years work! Four hundred new contacts in a pastor's cell phone, each representing a household unit that has attended at least one service—with the understanding that there are many others who don't give out their number to a preacher.

Over that first few months, W@W held a dinner every two weeks in which people could meet Jack, hear the vision, and ask questions, and it gave Jack the chance to get to know them better. He learned in those gatherings that about half the people came because they thought the beach was cool and liked the idea of worshiping there. The other half came because of a connection to Pastor Jack.

In late 2009, according to Kale, they made a mistake by trying to move the service across two long bridges all the way into Pensacola (a fifteen to thirty minute drive depending on traffic) in order to find a worship place more insulated from the weather. (The fall and winter winds can be sharp on this little stretch of the Gulf Coast.) After two months in Pensacola, with greatly reduced attendance, they decided to take a two-month sabbatical in January–February 2010, and then to start again in March 2010. They have not stopped since. For the year 2010 (March–December) good weather and bad, W@W averaged 333 in weekly attendance.

W@W now meets at 9:00 rather than 8:00 AM. They have packed up to four hundred people into the indoor portion of Flounders Restaurant when the weather was stormy or cold outdoors. In fact, the church installed flat screen TVs inside the restaurant and on the boardwalk outside so that folks could see what's going on even when their seating location was out of direct view of the worship leaders. But Jack says that on a lot of Sundays, even when it is quite chilly, people just wear coats, drink hot chocolate, and meet outdoors. In winter there are a lot of Sunday mornings on Pensacola Beach where 48 degrees or 50 degrees might be the lowest temperature—and so (with hot chocolate and low wind) it works.

As of this writing, the four hundred or so weekly worshipers are giving about $350,000 a year in donations to W@W. For a church this size, these are not huge numbers, less than $1000 a head annually. But we should remember that many of these folks are not traditional churchgoers. Also, it is notable that the budget for all costs (including Pastor Jack) at W@W was just over $100,000 last year. Talk about a ministry in the black!

As happens in church life, there was some controversy in the past couple years at one of the other campuses. This resulted in a precipitous decline in attendance and participation at that location. One of the upsides of a multisite ministry strategy is that some people can switch campuses to get some personal space, and they don't have to leave the church. W@W has certainly offered such space to a few folks from the other campus, so that Gulf Breeze Church was able to weather a storm in its life without taking as bad a hit overall as it would have taken in a more conventional one-campus situation.

During the BP Oil Spill in the summer of 2010, I turned on one of the national cable news channels. They were covering the oil spill story from Pensacola Beach on a Sunday morning. They suddenly cut to shots of faces I knew, and then the reporter said, "And one local church is on the beach praying the oil away." I laughed, because the TV news crew had missed the story. These were not desperate folks out on the beach to pray away oil for two or three weeks. This was a church, and the beach is their sanctuary, and they are there every Sunday, seeking to create a place where beach people can connect with the love and grace of God. The oil is gone now, but the Methodists haven't budged an inch.

In fact, on Easter Sunday morning in 2011, 853 worshipers gathered on that beach. And it had nothing to do with an oil spill. It had everything to do with the fact that Jack Kale refused to lead a dying church.

The most notable irony in this story is that Jack's own personal and theological shift in 2006 was related to an imbalanced emphasis on worship in the life of the church. And now he leads a thriving ministry called Worship @ the Water. This ministry took root when it became more than worship, but truly a community of faith. The worship did not really work here until the church was about more than simply worship.

But names stick and it is often hard to rebrand.

As is true of several of the stories in this book, the movement of God feels young on Pensacola Beach . . . they are just getting started. Their potential stretches far beyond what they have yet achieved. By the time you read this account, it may be somewhat out-of-date in terms of W@W's development, a bit like looking at pictures of your kids from two years ago. The community may take on a different name in time. It will certainly add ministries and initiatives far beyond what we have seen to date.

The group has begun an annual practice of pooling money as mission investors and then soliciting innovative ministry ideas, and the investors vote what new God-thing they want to fund. This kind of thinking is very promising for W@W, and it could lead them to significant mission achievement beyond worship in the years ahead.

15

THE REIMAGINED CHURCH

Sixth and I Historic Synagogue, Washington, D.C.

Three blocks from Calvary Baptist, on the other side of D.C.'s tiny Chinatown, there is a Jewish synagogue, named simply Sixth and I (prounounced "eye"; D.C. has lettered as well as numbered streets). Its red-tile domed roof is a neighborhood landmark. Built in 1907–8, this was the home of the Washington's Adas Israel congregation for forty-three years until they moved to their current location near the National Zoo, where they remain the largest Conservative synagogue in the city, with thousands of members and constituents.

You may recall from the Calvary story that this D.C. neighborhood has experienced a population turnover and major ethnic shift about every forty years. During the first half of the twentieth century, the neighborhoods that are today known as Penn Quarter and Mount Vernon Triangle formed the heart of the D.C. Jewish community, with people living in charming brick row houses and working downtown, often within walking distance of home. After World War II, the Jewish families shifted further northwest, building larger homes both in Washington and into the suburb of Bethesda. Meanwhile, the African American population in Washington was growing. The Shaw neighborhood (about a mile to the north of Sixth and I) had become the new black downtown in what was still a rather segregated city.

So Adas Israel sold the building at the corner Sixth and I in 1951 to Turner Memorial African Methodist Episcopal Church. Turner Memorial renovated the place and added a four-story activity building in the late seventies. Give it another forty years—and Turner's middle-class membership had steadily shifted toward Hyattsville, a suburb to the northeast. So in 2002 Turner Memorial announced plans to sell the Sixth and I property and move their church into the suburbs.

By this time, as I recounted in Calvary's story, downtown Washington had again become a focal zone for real estate development. Several Jewish businessmen were in the heart of the action. It had been apparent for some time that the dilapidated Penn Quarter neighborhood was occupying some of the most promising real estate in the world in the heart of America's capital city. In the eighties, while the neighborhood was still in rough condition, smart investors such as Douglas Jamal, Shelton Zuckerman, and Abe Pollin began buying up any property they could get their hands on in this zone.

In the nineties, Abe Pollin built what is now called the Verizon Center on two full city blocks and reestablished a Washington NBA franchise, the Washington Wizards. He even signed an aging Michael Jordan for the Wizards' first couple seasons to drum up local enthusiasm. Add to this that both the Georgetown NCAA basketball and the Washington Capitals hockey team made the Verizon their home arena. Untold thousands of people poured onto the streets several times each week. The neighborhood was hot again! The Verizon Center served as anchor for new cinemas, restaurants, and shopping in every direction, which in turn anchored the development of new apartments and luxury condos.

Georgetown University relocated its law school in the neighborhood. The new D.C. convention center opened at Mount Vernon Square. As I write this, the City Center project is underway at Ninth and H, the price tag of which will easily run past $2 billion.

Just up from City Center is the new flagship hotel for the Marriott Corporation (based in the D.C. area), under construction adjacent to the convention center.

I live in one of the condo high rises developed on land Doug Jamal owned. A freshman senator from Illinois named Obama lived in my building during his first year in Washington, even walking the half-mile to the Russell Senate Building on sunny days, without a security guard. The residents in my building tend to be young. I've been told almost half the units have either an attorney or a law student in residence.

Many of these new young Washingtonians are Jewish. And, as with other young American professionals, very few are active in the life of a faith community.

So ten years ago, when the new downtown was really beginning to pop and the old synagogue building went up for sale, people got to talking. Laura Cohen Applebaum, executive director of the Jewish Historical Society, was appalled by the rumor that the property might become a nightclub. She talked up the idea of making it a Jewish community center, a place that might fulfill the needs of young and unaffiliated Jews as they explore their Jewish identity. The property was complicated by the fact that it contained a historic structure in need of major (expensive) renovation and with considerable limitations on potential development.

Shelton Zuckerman looked at the building. He picked up the phone and called his friend Abe Pollin. The proposal: "I'll put $500K toward this, if you will, and we will find a third." This would take the property off the market; then, with the help of the wider D.C. Jewish community, they could gather up a board of directors and create a Jewish community center in the heart of the city. Abe Pollin wanted ten minutes to think about it. After ten minutes, he called back to say he was in. The two of them approached Doug Jamal about putting up the other third, and he agreed.

But here is where the story gets more interesting. Zuckerman is a Conservative Jew, and a member of Adas Israel. Abe Pollin was a Reformed Jew. And, as you might guess, Doug Jamal is Orthodox.

Three different denominations bought in to create the Sixth and I synagogue. In Christian terms, this would be like a liberal Protestant, an evangelical Protestant, and a Roman Catholic all going in together to build a center of faith community.

Obviously, with such diverse primary investors, the place was going to be nondenominational. (And we are not talking nondenominational in name only, like many American nondenominational churches, which are in fact more partisan and ideologically isolated than many modern denominations.) No, for this endeavor to work, it had to be a different kind of place altogether. And since clergy are often the ones who have the most difficult time working together across doctrinal lines, the place had to be run by laypeople. There could be no official ties or strings attached to any denomination or particular Jewish tradition. It would belong to the people. It will be managed independently.

So the investors created a diverse Jewish board of directors and hired an executive director. They renovated the sanctuary with donations from across the country, using photos from old wedding albums to guide them in historical details. Starting in 2004, the executive director then contracted with the various rabbis for them to come and hold services. Ultimately five different Jewish traditions came to hold services at Sixth and I, often simultaneously in different parts of the building, sometimes down the street at another house of worship. A sixth type of service utilizes a nondenominational prayer book and a band similar to contemporary forms of Protestant Christian worship.

The rabbis lead worship. They do not function in any sort of executive capacity. Some of them are on staff at other area synagogues. Some of them are bivocational. Some of them are not sure about others of them. Esther Foer, the current executive director, said, "Some of them (the clergy) may not even be sure they are going to see the others in heaven." But Sixth and I makes room for all Jewish traditions in its worship life, be they inclusive or exclusive in theological orientation.

In the early days, some major decisions had to be made beyond the fact that all types of Jewish traditions could be honored and practiced here. Among the biggest decisions:

- They had to rename the place. They chose Sixth and I because it was a neutral name, without undue religious baggage or connotation. "We had to pull people inside." This meant the name should not be too ethnic. They made the full name Sixth and I Historic Synagogue, thus claiming their most obvious asset—a fabulous, historic, centrally located building.

- They had to clarify their vision, which became "Where Jewish identity and community intersect." This would be a place for exploring Jewish identity and for offering community events that transcended an exclusively Jewish audience, but that featured prominent Jewish authors and artists. They summed it up like this: "As the place to be for innovative and re-imagined Jewish experiences, Sixth and I strives to be a welcoming gateway to Jewish life in downtown Washington, D.C."

- They had to decide that they would not compete with other excellent Jewish faith communities in Washington, but rather they would compete with the intellectual, social pull on D.C. people.

- They had to figure out how membership would work. Their answer: there would be no membership. Synagogue membership is an American innovation that dates back to Charleston, South Carolina, in 1824, when a local synagogue copied the Episcopalians in a plan to underwrite operating costs by renting pew space to families. Historically, synagogues were simply centers of Jewish life without membership and without emphasis on denomination. At Sixth and I, you do not have to be a donor to get a seat for High Holiday services. There is a small ticket-processing fee to insure that people don't reserve seats they don't plan to use. But anyone can get in—Jew or not.

- They had to figure out how to answer the cries of young adults for a sense of community and belonging, without membership. They realized that they would be in the business of constant community creation: sponsoring and birthing endless fellowships and gatherings that help participants forge relationships and discover a sense of interconnectedness.

- Without membership, fund-raising could become a challenge. So they had to create a funding plan that included large donations, profitable events, participant donations, and so on.

- They had to define their audiences. They use the concept of concentric circles. The innermost circle is made up of young Jews in D.C. The next circle out encompasses the broader D.C. Jewish community. Next circle out is the greater D.C. community who are interested in the arts, politics, ideas, and dialogue (including Gentiles like me). The widest circle out is the national Jewish community. (About half their participants live in the District of Columbia, and about half live in the suburbs—pretty typical for downtown D.C. faith communities.)

- They had to run a regional capital campaign in order to secure funding for the renovation of the facility.

- They had to figure out an organizational structure. They created a rather typical nonprofit structure with a board of directors hiring an executive director, which in turn hires staff, which in turn manages programming and volunteers.

When I went to interview executive director Esther Foer on a weekday afternoon, I looked around the modern, airy office at her staff—the whole place had a young, creative feel to it. She responded that one of their goals is to maintain a hip vibe, both in physical furnishings, in their printed materials and graphics, and in the creative edginess in their programming. The staff looked like the young condo-dwellers in the neighborhood. They were a little more conservatively dressed than those you might find in a dot-com business where people work in beanbag chairs, but the energy in the office was palpable. They have fun. They work for modest wages, often their first job out of college. They stay four or five years, often, because they enjoy the place and they are working in areas that relate to their personal values and passions.

Two of the staff persons are engaged full-time in financial development: one works full-time as a grant writer and the other manages donor relations. The rest create and manage various programs. I did not ask how many are on staff, but there were easily desks for a dozen people. Like the core community of volunteers and regular participants in Sixth and I life, the staff come from different parts of the nation, they are passionate about social justice, they desire authentic community, they are proud of being Jewish, and they do not necessarily define being Jewish in terms of a denomination.

They believe in cultivating good interfaith relationships—with Christians, with Buddhists, with Muslims. Sixth and I also works cooperatively with Christian faith communities in the neighborhood to support varied programs that address basic human need. The Dalai Lama was in D.C. the week that I was on the Sixth and I campus. Many people had come from afar, with small children, in order to share in an event with him. The synagogue provided childcare for Buddhist small children in their children's area for the duration of the event—a couple dozen kids each day. At the end of Ramadan last year, the synagogue hosted a breakfast meal for area Muslims.

The staff and the advisory team continue to generate new ideas for programming and community groups. At Sixth and I, though no one belongs to the synagogue itself, you can belong to a community within the system. One hundred fifty women belong to a young women's fellowship. Others belong to an interfaith couples group. There is a mother's circle with a twist: it's all non-Jewish women raising children as Jews, sort of "How to be a Jewish mother when you are not one." There are of course yoga groups, running groups, discussion and study groups. And new ones emerge all the time.

This synagogue does not want to become static. They feel a need to keep innovation at the forefront of things. So in 2011 the staff ran an ideas contest for what to do next. What is the next big idea? One hundred twenty-five persons made proposals, with a new iPad 2 as the prize for the winner. The winning entry was the idea of a Jewish food truck. In D.C., food trucks are the rage among downtown office workers and young professionals. People stand in line for half an hour when their favorite food truck comes up. We have food trucks in Washington with all sorts of ethnic food, but never had a Jewish food truck, until now.

Sixth and I staff now rent a food truck once a month and hang a banner over it called "Sixth and Rye." They chose traditional deli food (old-style Brooklyn food), found a rabbi from Baltimore to ride along and keep an eye on kosher requirements and practice, and people are talking. *The Huffington Post* covered them. They sell out in about two hours, with long lines every time. Each month, Sixth and Rye goes to a different place in the city. Each time, synagogue staffers go along in colorful t-shirts and work as greeters and ambassadors for Sixth and I during the two hours.

I wondered aloud how financially sustainable Sixth and I is, with no membership and such a young constituency. I learned that each year, they get closer to paying all of their expenses from a combination of ticket sales for special events and current-year donations and long-term endowment interest. The key: Eight thousand people a month gather for something at Sixth and I. The eight-hundred-seat sanctuary is filled to capacity at least once each week, and sometimes twice, with services, community gatherings, concerts, lectures, and so forth. Some events are directed at smaller audiences. Weekly volume of people is the key, not the size of particular events.

Their budget is only about $1.5 million, which is amazing given all they do with the money. The money is spent on religious programming, staff, and the building. That is slightly less than my church's budget; yet these people run circles around us in terms of sheer creativity of programming and the numbers of people moving in and out their doors. They also typically work on a shoestring budget, even for big events. Simplicity in their events helps to insure a profit margin.

About sixty percent of persons who attend their religious services are unaffiliated with any faith community. They are achieving their mission.

On a typical Sabbath, you might walk in to see a simple traditional service, a yoga-infused service, or a female rabbi leading a musical service with a band.

Here is the range of worship options in a typical week:

- Open Space: times for contemplation and reflection are offered throughout Rosh Hashanna and Yom Kippur.

- Sixth in the City Service: a spirited service for young professionals blending old and new traditions—held on Friday evenings *at Calvary Baptist.* They sponsor an annual Rosh Hashanah retreat with hiking, singing, prayer, and picnic.

- Traditional Service

- Explanatory Service: Traditional service with commentary geared toward young professionals. Separate seating for men and women.

- Preschool Service: Interactive service with music, energy, and fun for families with small children: Saturday mornings at Calvary Baptist.

- Special Kids Services at Rosh Hashanah (a lunchtime multicultural Seder for children ages six through eleven) and at Yom Kippur (focusing on Jewish values and ethics).

I sense that the business model of Sixth and I would collapse were it not for the volume of people they run through their doors, and the people would dry up were it not for the big names and high quality programming that they offer. All of their nonreligious programming generates a profit, just as if they were a local theater center. If I were to contemplate doing such a thing as this with a Protestant identity (and I might at some point), I think I would want to work with someone who knew how to manage and program a theater center. They would know how to book the big names, price the event, do the PR, staff everything, and show a profit week after week, so as to underwrite the religious activities that may never pay for themselves with an audience of largely transient young adults. I would also want to work with someone who knew how to raise money.

You can't pull off something like Sixth and I and think small or think less than first class. This place happened because of the convergence of several big thinkers who painted in large brush strokes. They did things well, and they did them large.

So I look on the wall in the synagogue visitor lounge at pictures of the people who have been booked at Sixth and I in the last few years, many of them Jews, but not all: Toni Morrison, Annie Liebovitz, Nancy Pelosi, Tom Brokaw, Elizabeth Gilbert (*Eat, Pray, Love*), Salmon Rushdie, John Kerry, George W. Bush, Chris and Kathleen Matthews, Ruth Bader Ginsburg, and even sex guru Dr. Drew. Big names. Many of Sixth and I's special guests, artists, and speakers are able to come through partnerships with other organizations, such as the National Geographic Society, D.C.'s famous Politics and Prose bookstore, *Slate* magazine, *The New Republic*, Live Nation (concert bookers), and others. With a relatively small staff, Sixth and I depends on such partnerships to book their talent.

One of my first times to Sixth and I was to hear *New York Times* columnist Tom Friedman talk about his sequel to his best seller *The World is Flat*. I discovered my down-the-hall neighbors (from my building) sitting on the same row. We scooted together and chatted. It felt almost small town. In the fall of 2008, I went to an election night party, with burgers, drinks, big screen TVs, and live commentary by local political scientists on what was happening as election returns were announced. At one point, I saw the film *The Kite*

Runner here. A few months back, I attended the showing of a documentary on the lives of undocumented immigrants. Through such events, I feel a part of the Sixth and I community, and also more a part of my community in downtown Washington.

As the Sixth and I community matures, young adults who became involved are now getting married and having children. The community is beginning to reflect a multigenerational reality. Weddings have been a big business for years, but now there is growing interest in bris, naming ceremonies, mitzvahs, family reunions, funerals, and other major events in people's lives. Classes abound with all ages, ranging from eight weeks of introductory Hebrew to "How to Make Sushi."

Before his death, Abe Pollin reflected, "I have been involved in a few projects in my life, but never, ever have I been involved in a project that means as much to me and my family as this project has."

Esther Foer steps back and says: "I marvel at how this place consistently bridges its historical, physical grandeur with cutting-edge programs that are equally stunning in substance and significance. The hundreds of young people who visit Sixth and I night after night symbolize the future of American Jewry."

Some of you may have wondered at first why the story of a Jewish synagogue's rebirth made it into a book whose audience consists mostly of leaders in Christian churches. Most of you now see why—but in case you don't, let me underline the point: stories like Sixth and I bust wide and free of the patterns that typify the other stories—and they illustrate how vast the possibilities are. It is not so much what they did, but the way that they stepped beyond so many conventional assumptions to do it—that is what I want you to take away from their story.

I hope that you will walk away from this book with several new ideas for rethinking your church's path forward in relationship with its community. But I do not want you to limit your thinking based upon what somebody else tried or upon conventional thinking.

I have never written a 1-2-3, how-to-grow-a-church book, and I never will. The Book of Acts is too dynamic for such a spiritless approach to life. The Sixth and I team demonstrates the dynamic nature of faith community development perhaps more than any other group in this book. They know that they cannot build their success on the patterns or formulas of other people in other places. They can learn from any and all, but finally, they understand that God gave them brains and hearts and eyes and ears and resources, in order for them to come together and figure what will work for their community in this time, as they live into the vision of who God has called them to be.

I invite you and your cohorts at your church to do this.

I invite you to test all of your assumptions and to really think outside the box. I invite you to ask, yet again, what business are you in, ultimately. I invite you to work with more blank pages and fewer templates! I invite you to engage your unaffiliated neighbors in serious conversation and ministry collaboration to bless your community.

And I invite you to bathe it all in a trust that God will show you some mighty things if you keep your eyes open—things that may surprise you, delight you, scare you, and certainly energize you for a new century of witness and service that is unlike any time that has come before.

The majority of the current congregations in America will die before the year 2100. That's a fair bet. But there are very few cases where this is inevitable. We can choose another storyline with God.

Take inspiration from these, your spiritual co-laborers in other fields and in other traditions. Then go home. Go home, and find some kindred spirits in the place that you call church, or in the larger community where you live, and start dreaming with God! If you can't figure out anything else to do, just start praying together, week after week, talking with one another and with God, and asking God to show you new possibilities.

Since I was a very young man, one of my favorite verses in the Hebrew Scripture comes from the Book of Isaiah, chapter 43, verse

7, where God says, "Behold I am doing a new thing! Now it springs up! Do you not perceive it? I am making a way in the desert and springs in the wasteland."

The best faith community stories of the twenty-first century are almost all yet to be written. I write books such as this in the hope and the faith that some of you who read these pages will step up to write some of those stories!

There is a story of good news in community that *you and your friends* are meant to tell. It is a story unlike any other that can ever be lived or told. You and your church are the only ones who can tell it.

And our world is dying for such good news.

흐

16

EPILOGUE: A CONVERSATION

Paul Nixon with
Charlene Kammerer,
Christie Latona,
Martin Lee, and
Rita Root

PAUL—Friends, thank you for sinking your teeth into these stories and agreeing to share in conversation about the issues they raise. The four of you make for an amazing "dinner party." You are all people of powerful ideas and action—and I am sure you could tell another fifteen stories each from the churches where you have worked as judicatory leaders and as ministry coaches.

Some of these stories may remind you of some of the churches with which you have worked. Where did you have a déjà vu moment as you read these stories?

CHARLENE—Several of these stories of congregations who "gave away" their substance reminded me of a congregation's choice earlier in my ministry. The church is Wesley Memorial United Methodist Church in Ft. Myers, Florida. In working with the team on missions, I suggested one year that we ask the finance committee to commit 100 percent of any reserve funds at year's end to the work of missions—locally, nationally, and globally. This "giving away" of our reserve funds caused quite a stir among some of our parishioners. The finance council narrowly approved the recommendation. Word got out all around the church community about what was going on. Weekly giving began to go up; conversation about hands-on mission increased at all age levels. At year's end, the finance councile announced that tens of thousands of dollars were available in reserve spending for missions. A new spirit of excitement, commitment, and service unfolded in the life of the church. It was one of the most fruitful years of ministry there and sparked new mission partnerships.

MARTIN—There are so many churches like First United Methodist Church in Sikeston, Missouri. They are not able to open up and see new things. In many cases they would rather die silently than go through change. But, two things made a difference here: leadership and prayer. I see in this story what I see in all successful faith community redevelopments: every time they began something, they started with a prayer. Every discussion began with prayer. Every church could do this but many don't. I believe that there's no other way to empty our ego. Ego is edging God out and then putting oneself in, and I believe prayer helps us to empty our ego and discern God's will. This is a very strong congregation with a strong ego. Through the prayer team, they were able to set the new ground rules, move forward, and grow. Prayer helps meet God's possibilities. "When we work, we work; but when we pray, God works," said Max Lucado.

RITA—Martin, I still see Darlene Kelley up in the organ pipes praying, with the chains around her neck. That was the turning point at Clinton Avenue.

In terms of déjà vu, I have seen huge smiles and deep sighs of relief when, after asking what the biggest challenges are and hearing "not enough people to sit on our committees, I've said "get rid of the committees." Several of these stories breathed with relief around the creation of a fresh, sensible, workable organizational life.

The story of the attempted coup by a staff member whose family were influential members of the church was personally painful; I am a pastor who survived a similar "season of mutiny." The silver lining was a doctoral dissertation on leading a church through conflict and a congregation who found the courage not to be bullied. Church revitalization is not for the faint of heart. It is important that you know deep down that it isn't about you, especially when everyone (even those who support you) wants to make it about you. I read lots of Edwin Friedman's work on self-differentiation during that season. You are neither as awful nor as wonderful as people say you are.

PAUL—Amen to Ed Friedman.

CHRISTIE—It's funny: every church's journey is just so distinct. Since leadership style and congregational context determine how transformation flows, no single story paralleled my experiences with any single congregation. But I see in these stories *hallmarks* of transformational leaders (lay and clergy) who:

- Raise expectations
- Hit the ground running (although timing differs)
- Model behaviors they wish to see
- Don't run from pivotal truth-telling meetings
- Engage in intense and intentional prayer
- Respond to external crises well and together
- Create unity and convergence by pointing the congregation to the movement of God
- Adjust structure to fit the vision/direction and free up people and control
- Create more positive visibility in the community

PAUL—I feel like you just described Evangel Church in Holton, Kansas. They are like the poster child of the hallmarks you list.

CHRISTIE—Absolutely! I saw most hallmarks in the other stories too but they may have been more difficult to see because of the timeline, leadership style, number of people involved, or context. The gift you've given in this diversity of storytelling is that you've illustrated how transformation feels and looks different.

PAUL—Christie has shared these hallmarks of transformation experiences where she has worked. What about the rest of you? *As you have worked to help churches choose life across the years, how does any of this illustrate key learning for you?*

CHARLENE—Three things come to mind: first, leadership (both lay and clergy) is key in leading a church to new life, or vital transformation. Second, a "vital congregation" doesn't have to be a large membership church. These stories illustrate that fact. Growing spiritually and numerically doesn't always mean that it will be heading toward a megachurch reality. Third, congregations can be progressive in their social stances and involvement in the wider community and grow. Some people will never associate with any church unless it is meaningfully involved in the neighborhood beyond its walls. A church committed to modeling inclusivity in membership and radical hospitality has a strong chance to grow and impact a neighborhood or a region. These stories offer proof that this is possible.

RITA—I believe that pastoral leadership is key, both in terms of finding the right match, and also in terms of doing good transition work. I want to commend the way that United Christian refused to settle for the best they could find in their denominational system, when the person they needed was outside the conventional boundaries—and in fact outside their denominational body. As a judicatory official in a system that is congregational in polity, I occasionally watch churches do just this—and it can be a brilliant move.

Also, I liked the way that Kent Rogers at Evangel approached his work exactly like a good intentional interim. That was not what they appointed him to be, but in fact that is how he went in: asking the right questions and expecting action to be taken in response to the gathered information. It was risky, and yet, the first year, that dicey transitional year, became the platform on which Kent and Evangel then built a healthy and fruitful ministry partnership.

At St. Mark, Telley Gadsen evoked—she called forth—a vision that lay dormant within the church membership. So often, this is the pastor's challenge—to pour water on the seeds of good faith and heritage that exists deep in the hearts, minds, and memories of a congregation, and reanimate it!

Other things that I have learned that I see illustrated in these stories would be:

- In-between time—time in the wilderness—is important, a time when a fresh sense of congregational identity and vision can be forged.

- Authentic community, deep spirituality, and embodied justice are what draw people to progressive communities of faith.

- Sometimes, even we offer a church a way forward that is the best chance of survival, some folks will choose to let the congregation die rather than change (thinking of the church in Sumter, South Carolina, that resisted the merger).

- It used to be location, location, location. Now it is radical welcome, radical welcome, radical welcome.

MARTIN—And leadership, leadership, leadership.

PAUL—Martin, you are the third in a row to lead your remarks here with a comment about the importance of leadership. I think that tells us something.

MARTIN—Over the years I've learned that every congregation goes through a crisis from time to time, and it's necessary to take it as an opportunity. The Chinese word for crisis is made from the combination of two symbols. One is "danger" and one is "opportunity." Put together they form "crisis." As a leader, whenever you see a crisis, you have to think that there is an opportunity.

Take, for example, the story of Evangel United Methodist Church. There was a huge snowstorm and the whole community was without power. Because the church was able to get electricity back and running before its neighbors, it provided shelter for the whole community. Sometimes if you want to grow a church, you have to expend some miracles—in this case using the crisis as a way to change people's minds about the church.

When a crisis happens, it's up to the clergy and laity to see it as opportunity rather than as a danger. When church leadership grasps the opportunity, they can move to the next level, a healthier level for the congregation.

A crisis can also help you to see new possibilities. Lake Alfred Presbyterian Church suffered from a series of hurricanes, and the sanctuary was destroyed. Because of the circumstances they had to move worship to the fellowship hall—it was the beginning of an opening process. Seeing a crisis as an opportunity, that makes a difference. If you don't do it, God sometimes will open the door for you, sending a storm.

CHRISTIE—I totally agree with you, Martin. Transformation is a faith decision. I can testify to the fact that transformation will come to pass when key leaders are fully surrendered to seek and do God's will—to align the ministry with the Great Commandment and Commission in their context. Paul, I strongly affirm your statement, "Seek ye first the reign of God and attendance and money will care for themselves." We have to stop trusting our logic and emotions more than God. I hope people see the variety of shape this takes and are encouraged to start or continue their own congregation's transformation story. This is illustrated in most vibrantly at Clinton Avenue, Montavilla, and Sag Harbor.

Also, a written vision statement isn't as important as a powerful, personal, and pervasive understanding of who we are and who we are called to be in the community. Many of these stories lived their way to the point that they could put a vision statement together. It didn't start with the vision that could fit on a t-shirt. That was just an outward, visible sign that convergence of purpose had occurred. It often takes talking and acting before any stating of purpose is meaningful.

PAUL—People reading this, please circle the preceding paragraph!

CHRISTIE—In interviews with exemplary Romans 12 project congregations, we discovered every pastor revealed that she or he had at least one powerful partner (lay or clergy) who had linked arms with her or him. Some of the stories you told mentioned key partners, but I would imagine that every one of these pastors had such partners. Another finding that showed up your stories was prayer as a central, decision-making, and decision-confirming tool.

PAUL—*As you read the stories, were there one or two big ideas that began to echo within your head?*

MARTIN—Change is very, very difficult. Whether the congregation is large or small, change means growing pains. A church cannot grow without growing pains. True leadership can help a congregation see the current reality and envision their bright future. Throughout the process, leadership is critical.

Every congregation featured in this book opened up their hearts and minds to their community, which means that they are able to see the needs of their community. In many cases the community changes—racial, economic, all kinds of changes happen—and the church is not able to see the changes. Churches do not see their surrounding neighbors and the neighbors don't see the church either. That is the reality of many congregations today.

CHARLENE—A church can choose to embrace new life. This will often necessitate some members leaving, new leaders emerging, a change in pastor, a redesign of the facility, and a commitment to be welcoming of ALL and to offer the grace and love of Christ unconditionally. A denomination can be in a posture of holy listening; it can offer training and peer support for the pastor and also offer grants for discerned facility or ministry needs within the church at a critical point of time.

PAUL—Choosing life over death is foundational to all the other good choices that may come.

CHRISTIE—I think the power in these stories is how they help us more deeply understand the difference between a church that embraces life and one that ultimately chooses something else. These stories show that is not a matter of resources or extraordinary circumstances or specific universal steps. It is about determination, character, subordination to the Great Commandment and Commission, and ultimately working to make the church a resource to its community. Each story had a different starting point and illustrates the diversity in how God's people sought God's will and guidance in the transformation process.

Choosing life is chaotic, nonlinear, and joyful and will contain pain of one type or another. It also isn't just one choice or one moment. It is an ongoing journey! Several of these stories show that brilliantly. Yet just when it gets messier than we could have ever imagined, transformation is around the corner.

Throughout the reading, I wanted to pray for those leaders who walk into conflict-soaked places. It takes longer, it is much more taxing, and it requires a thicker skin and greater faith than most of us have.

RITA—As I read the Sixth and I story, I thought, "People long to know who they are and to be in places where they can bring their full and authentic selves." In almost every story, the church found a fresh way to embrace their communities authentically and to tell people who they are.

We heard about quite a few church buildings that had been flagships and now were museums or sagging ruins. The majority of these churches made bold moves with regard to their relationship to their sacred space—whether it meant selling the building, repurposing it, or creating alliances with others in order to be good stewards of the square footage.

Another big idea that hangs with me is this: Give it away—give all of it away! Shift your focus from "what will it take to survive" and focus on what is life-giving for other people now. Trust that what is needed is already there among you!

PAUL—*Where, in reading these stories, did any of you laugh out loud?*

MARTIN—Two places in particular. When it took snakes finally to get a church to relocate (when they had needed to for some time) and when the TV crew misinterpreted a church's worship service as a prayer meeting that someone would come clean up the oil spill.

CHRISTIE—God does have a sense of humor! I had to laugh when I read about the pastor singing selections from *Les Mis.* I have seen pastors seek to make their preaching relevant in lots of ways, but that takes the cake.

PAUL—In his defense, I judge an interim pastorate by how good a platform is set for the permanent pastor—and in this case, the interim gets an A . . . show tunes and all!

RITA—I laughed out loud in thinking about the new Chestnut Street Memorial and Museum that could have been built, had Chestnut Street moved too quickly to create a new space before they had taken time (in their three years at the synagogue) to grieve the ending of one era and to think more clearly about what they wanted the next to be.

PAUL—Yes, I saw a church rebuild too quickly once, and the new multipurpose facility looked like Grandma's country house, entirely unsuitable for the people that church wanted and needed to reach.

RITA—Also, the vote that almost happened at United Christian about whether or not to practice weekly communion—I laughed because from a distance it seems so ridiculous. Thank goodness for the pastor who could see clearly up close to the controversy, and who wisely acted to avoid that showdown!

CHARLENE—Paul, the places I laughed out loud was where your voice, your sense of humor came through. That is sprinkled throughout the stories. The telling of the stories themselves did not make me laugh, sometimes made me cry, and often made me prayerfully thankful. But I appreciate your humor in the telling of the stories!

PAUL—Thank you, Charlene.

Stories sometimes raise as many questions as they answer. *Where are you asking questions right now as you think about church development? Where are you wondering, and perhaps sensing that we don't know as much as we like to think we know about any of this?*

CHARLENE—In thinking about church development, I am asking two questions these days: First, what is the tipping point for a congregation to choose to die to the past and claim a new future given to them by God? Here in Virginia Methodism, too many people have a sense of being comfortable where they are, in their church, in their town, in their history and present, to risk becoming something better, even for the glory of God. Another question: How can we help raise critical dollars for this work when everyone is not on board with the goal of vital congregations?

CHRISTIE—At the judicatory, regional, and national levels that question is huge and more complex than I have experienced at the local church level, where one can paint a more specific, compelling vision about what God is calling a congregation to be. I know many denominational leaders are seeking to raise up strong "turnaround" pastors. How should what Paul has put before us inform our approach to identifying and calling/appointing/assigning "turnaround" pastors? I'm guessing that some of these leaders surprised the person who hired them.

PAUL—I am guessing you are right about that.

CHRISTIE—Viewed from the outside, most of these places looked hopeless or on the way out. Yet each had a game-changing moment that happened when a spiritual leader was at the wheel in a place with some good spiritual bones. How often are we closing places that could have had a second life? How often are we leaving churches open or independent when we need a takeover or vital merger?

MARTIN—My questions relate to the deployment of laity (persons who have not been ordained as pastors) as leaders, particularly in the United Methodist context. They're one of our best assets, but how can we use them as part of a new ministry? First, how can we mobilize and utilize lay ministers in our system? Second, how do we recruit more passionate lay ministers? Third, how do we find passionate local partners to team with those assigned to lead, so that renewed ministry can happen in some of these places?

RITA—I want to know how we might stop pouring so many resources into crumbling buildings and restoring "world-class" organs from another era?

PAUL—For every church that does what Calvary did to its building (and at astronomical cost) and comes back, many more throw the money like a big Vegas bet into the building and then lose the church anyway.

RITA—Totally! Too often, I hear the commitment to stay the same until the endowment runs out and the last member turns off the lights. It's painful. How can we preserve some of these resources for more effective investment in building new faith community in these places?

PAUL—In Calvary's case I am glad they made the investment to renew their presence in my neighborhood. Yet I also know there is another church within three blocks that made a similar investment to renovate their building. Both churches are growing, but they also could fit easily within either building, with room to spare for hundreds of new people! So there is a stewardship issue here, certainly.

Was there any story where you wanted to speak, as an encourager to the church or the leaders?

CHRISTIE—I felt compelled to speak a word of encouragement to Amy at Calvary. From the ghost of the former pastor to the sexism to the coup to the family repercussions, she has had to develop deeper spiritual roots and tougher skin. I wanted to encourage her to praise God for delivering her through all of this and to thank her for her faithfulness. I wanted to congratulate her for taking the time to care for herself and her spirit and encourage her to do even more of it. I also felt compelled for her to be less hard on herself (from the Easter story I suspect she may have a little perfectionist in her) and to take every opportunity to enjoy the journey.

CHARLENE—Honestly, I found myself wanting to say to them all, especially pastors, "Go for it! I see God working powerfully through you and your people. Trust your future—it is in God's hands. Thank you for the inspiration you are providing for so many of us, even if you don't realize that."

As a bishop, I would also like to suggest to each pastor to invest in a relationship with his or her supervisor, whoever that is in their church polity. You have much to teach us and I believe there will be more support that you might expect from your denominational partners.

PAUL—In Amy's case, there wasn't much there in supervisory support—just the nature of Baptist polity. But she did get a spiritual director and a coach—and both were really critical in helping her keep on through the toughest season.

MARTIN—Two places where I wanted to cheer for the leaders were Irvine United Congregational Church and Sixth and I Synagogue. In the first case, leaders spoke truth boldly, resulting in a public witness, but also in a series of persons, who were feeling squeezed out by other churches, finding a spiritual home at Irvine UCC. In the latter case, the Sixth and I team created such amazing space and opportunity for the community to mingle together. In the United States, religion is often more of a source of tension than a source of growth and mutual respect. The fact that thousands of religious and nominally religious people could come together and experience a sense of community around Jewish identity is inspiring.

RITA—I wanted to cheer for the folks at Lake Alfred who decided it was okay to be a church of older adults! It is more than okay! To each of the churches: Be who you are right now—don't try to reshape everything to be the church you think you are supposed to be!

I felt uplifted by the statement that Irvine UCC allowed people to leave "quietly and respectfully." It is such a simple thing, but we should try to part by blessing one another whenever we can!

I was delighted to read that Tom came to Sag Harbor as a certified lay speaker! Go Tom!! Good for Tom, good for the church, and good for the cabinet that made this assignment! As financial resources dwindle for our congregations, the ability to think beyond the traditional seminary-trained ordained pastor can refocus the ministry and reenergize the laity.

PAUL—*What other issues are on your mind in the wake of reading this book?*

CHARLENE—I wonder why so many of these pastoral leaders named in this book are women. Does it have to do with the fact that women are willing to serve in places that their male peers are not? Does it have to do with being willing to accept lower salaries in tough situations? Do women's life experiences of sacrificing to bring new life into the world help them as pastors to appreciate the struggle, pain, and opportunity that churches on the brink of dying represent?

Another question: Where are the voices of the youth and young adults in these stories? I would like to hear more about the next generation's perspective on willingness to invest in bringing congregations to new life.

PAUL—Your question about youthful voices makes me think. In each of the church interviews, we talked first with the pastor and then with a group of leaders chosen by the pastor. Only Telley Gadson invited high school students to the latter conversation. But there were young adults in several of the groups who told me the tales of their church's journey toward life. A few of these churches lowered the median age of their participants by over fifty years!

Recently I spent three days in a conflicted North Carolina congregation, allowing about one hundred folks to debrief about what was going on in their church. There were two groups that stood out from the others, groups that were full of joy, living almost in a parallel reality to the issues that were consuming and dividing the rest of the church—first the high school students in a healthy youth ministry, and then the parents of those same young people. This reminded me that, for good or for bad, young people often live among us with a different focus and a different storyline. In the North Carolina church, they were simply focused on the joy of discovering God's grace personally, learning how to serve others and to be a part of making a good difference in the world.

MARTIN—Every person is part of a whole under God, and one person missing leaves a gap. Every person matters to God. I still want to believe the church is the hope of the world. For this to be so, we have to create spaces where people are accepted and blessed as they are, places where they can fully recognize their potential as precious human beings.

CHRISTIE—I am left thinking about how I might use this resource in my work. In working with local churches, I might pick the one church from this book that seems most relevant to their situation and use that story (1) to help them better understand their stuck place, (2) to help them name an elephant in the room, or (3) to open them up to think imaginatively about what possibilities God is waiting to reveal.

RITA—I keep thinking about how much prayer and work went in to these stories. These were not one-hour-a-week projects!

PAUL—Rita, it was a lot of work just getting them on paper—but the people who actually lived these stories—wow! It was a major gift of time and love in every case, by a good cast of characters, more lay than clergy.

RITA—One hour on Sunday morning—even the well-crafted hour possible—is not enough to engage the imagination and commitment of persons who wish to live full and engaged lives. Even less is it enough to enable us to vision well as a church or to serve our neighbors faithfully. *We have to be more than one-hour-a-week faith communities!*

I also want to note the intentional and radical hospitality shown to the queer community in about half of these stories. Did you look for that specifically in your search for good stories?

PAUL—I did not look for any particular elements in these stories except that the churches were almost dead—or in a couple instances, so stuck as to be as good as dead—and then something happened and now they are profoundly alive. I turned to denominational officials for nominees all over America. This collection of stories is a snapshot of what church transformation looks like in mainline congregations, without regard for their positions (or lack of positions) on LGBT inclusion.

CHRISTIE—Paul, I have a question for you: why did you choose the Calvary story to lead the book? I found it to be really painful to read—in fact it sort of threw me back rather than inspiring me forward.

PAUL—I could have led with any of these stories. The Calvary story moved me more deeply, though, than any other. Much of that story unfolded behind the church's red brick walls while I was happily chugging coffee at Starbucks and eating pizza at Matchbox right across the street! I had no idea. I knew the church was on a comeback journey, but the rest was unknown to all us folks who passed outside every day, and unknown to many of the new worshipers on the inside! I was dizzy by the time the interviews were done there.

I put their story up front because it said so well what often is forgotten in an era where baby boomers have set the theme and tone of American Christianity—it reminds us that, finally, we follow a suffering servant Savior. Whether we are helping to bring new life to old churches or to change bedpans, servanthood sometimes just stinks. My father (pre–baby boom) was a pastor who suffered in his ministry—there were times when he hated it, when the only thing that kept him in it was the sense that God was calling him, and he really had no choice but to follow and to be faithful. When he found out I was going to become a pastor, he wanted to throw up. Seriously. He knew things. And he had managed to hide me from much of what he knew as I grew up richly blessed in the churches he served so well!

The kind of suffering that Amy (and a few others in this book) endured in the rebirthing of a church is just plain distasteful. But there is a good "cloud of witnesses" who have gone before us— colleagues in the faith in earlier times and in other parts of the world—who paid a price that twenty-first-century North American Christians might consider extreme. Many pastors have come to expect from ministry a fulfilling career, with lots of warm fuzzies and good opportunities for self-actualization.

If I could conjure up a dead person to add to this conversation, it would be Carlyle Marney, who mentored one of the people who mentored me. Marney, in one of his unpublished sermons, quotes John Bunyan from *Pilgrim's Progress* as a way of touching upon what it means to be a pastor: "He is called One of a Thousand; he is a begetter of spiritual children; He is a birther, he is a nurse; he knows and unfolds dark things to sinners. He pleads, he slights and despises the things that are present, and he is sure of a world to come."* Granted, it is a grim depiction of the pastoral task, almost echoing that morbid character on *Saturday Night Live*, Debbie Downer. But I think it stands as a good counterbalance to the spirit of our era and the naïve expectations of many who enter this work.

Each of you has been through parenthood, including adolescence and some painful moments in the journey of birthing and guiding your children to maturity—I think there is some parallel. I am going to guess we all lost a little sleep along the way with kids. So you tell me, "Was it worth it?"

MARTIN—We have two children, ages twenty-four and eighteen—quite an age gap because we had a miscarriage. If because of the experience of miscarriage we had given up, we would never have known the joy of our second child, whom, we in fact named, Joy. Birthing new life, be it in the context of faith community or in our families—this is holy work.

CHARLENE—In answering a call to ordained leadership in the church, you can't possibly know what you are saying YES to. This

---

*Michael C. Blackwell, "Carlyle Marney as Ethicist," *Christian Ethics Today* 17 (August 1998), 18.

was a leap of faith like no other in my life ... until I became a parent! My husband, Leigh, and I were married ten years before becoming parents, and we finally adopted a baby boy through a miraculous circumstance. We thought we would be so ready because we had yearned to be parents for so long. But we had no idea what we were saying YES to. It took all the courage and energy we could give to raising our little boy, Christopher. We had to juggle child-care, times when Christopher was sick, school schedules, work schedules, and so on. Vacation times were often interrupted with church crises or needs for his parents to weigh in. But over a sustained period of time, our investment in raising our son bore fruit. We could not be prouder of our son, now thirty-two and in the US Navy, a father of three, and a decent and loveable man. He is a special child of God. We named him Christopher because he represented Christ's love to us the moment he entered into our lives at four days old. Over thirty-seven years of ministry, of tending and nurturing congregations, of tending my own spiritual life, of providing spiritual administration as district superintendent and bishop, I have seen God's gracious Spirit bear fruit in the lives of people and churches. There is much I haven't seen and will never know, but I trust God the Gardner to reveal the fruit. Thanks be to God!

CHRISTIE—Being a parent is definitely worth it! And I agree that it is holy work that takes courage and faith. I have three teenagers and have experienced more than my share of joy. I feel blessed (and at times unworthy) to be the mom of such spectacular beings. But as anyone with teenagers knows, there have been seasons of deep sorrow, seasons when I felt like the floor had been pulled out from under me. Just as pastors mourn and go into a period of reflection when their spiritual children don't resemble what they hoped for, I have mourned each time my children have made choices that Peter and I didn't want for them. It is only in my experiencing of the Holy Spirit praying for me, Jesus guiding me, and God holding me have I made it through those teenage traumas and emerged with a better understanding of my place in the world and the fact that God is in control. I do think this is parallel to how successful pastors make it through the trials of birthing new life and then guiding it to maturity by giving it to God.

OTHER BOOKS FROM THE PILGRIM PRESS

FINDING JESUS ON THE METRO
And Other Surprises Doing Church in a New Day
PAUL NIXON
978-0-8298-1854-3/paper/144 pages/$14.00

Finding Jesus on the Metro explores what it means for a church to be on a ministry journey into the unchartered territory of unprecedented social change in twenty-first century America. Written from an urban perspective, Nixon has created an excellent tool for church leaders that (1) helps them to recognize that their ministry must change in order to be effective and (2) equips them with the necessary resources to implement and cultivate this change.

I REFUSE TO LEAD A DYING CHURCH
PAUL NIXON
978-0-8298-1759-1/paper/128 pages/$16.00

"God has called all leaders, lay and clergy, to lead healthy, growing spiritual movements. For this reason, I refuse to lead a dying church. And I invite you . . . to join me in refusing, ever again, to lead a dying church."
—from the introduction

THE CHURCH MOUSE
Leadership Lessons from the Magic Kingdom
CHRISTOPHER W. PERRY
978-0-8298-1874-1/paper/192/$22.00

Disney attracts millions of people to its parks each year. Millions more watch its shows, buy its merchandise, and flock to its animated movies. What makes Disney different from all other competitors? In *The Church Mouse: Leadership Lessons from the Magic Kingdom*, Christopher Perry examines the principles that for years have separated Disney from others in the entertainment industry and applies these principles to the church. Readers will gain new insight into intentionally building a church culture, creating excitement, developing leaders, and unleashing the creative potential of all members.

LEARNING TO TALK SHEEP
Understanding Those You Lead
CHRISTOPHER W. PERRY AND C. WAYNE PERRY
978-0-8298-1850-5/paper/144 pages/$18.00

Based on more than ten years of research, *Learning to Talk Sheep* uses the common biblical image of the people of God as sheep and the pastor as their shepherd to describe the major types of personalities and members that every pastor will encounter. It offers guidance for pastors and lay leaders to work more efficiently and effective with those they lead.

To order these or any other books from The Pilgrim Press call or write to:

THE PILGRIM PRESS
700 PROSPECT AVENUE EAST
CLEVELAND, OHIO 44115-1100

Phone orders: 1-800-537-3394　■　Fax orders: 216-736-2206

Please include shipping charges of $6.00 for the first book and $1.00 for each additional book.

Or order from our web sites at www.thepilgrimpress.com and www.ucpress.com.

Prices subject to change without notice.